Sharing Jesus with Under Fives

How to reach young children with the gospel

Janet Gaukroger

**published by
Christian Focus Publications**

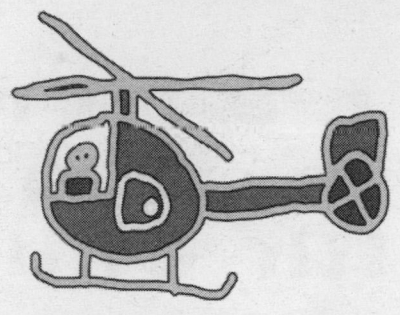

©copyright 2001 Janet Gaukroger
Published by Christian Focus Publications
Geanies House, Fearn, Tain
Ross-shire, Scotland, U.K., IV20 1TW
www.christianfocus.com
email: info@christianfocus.com
ISBN: 1-85792-672-2

Printed and bound in Omnia, Bishopbriggs,
Glasgow, Scotland

Cover design by Alister Macinnes

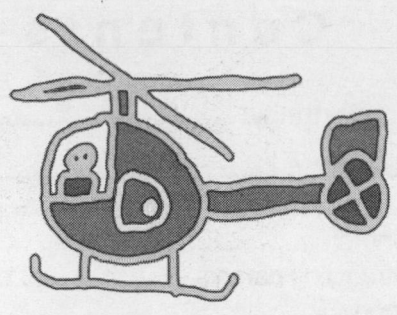

We're never too young to learn about Jesus!
In her book, *Sharing Jesus with under fives*, Janet gives
wisdom-packed ways of doing just that.
This is a book filled with pearls of wisdom, based on
Janet's long term experience in dealing with children
under five at Sunday School. She speaks from the heart
of her longing to see under fives understand the
esssence of the Christian faith.
Fiona Castle

A very timely and most helpful presentation
that fills a need... long overdue. This has been done by
one of the ablest Christian women in Britain.
R T Kendall

A practical handbook to help you invest in the future.
Rob Parsons,
Care for the Family

JANET GAUKROGER

Janet has over 20 years experience of teaching children
under five in church. She also speaks on child and family
issues at conventions, such as Spring Harvest, and
conducts regional seminars about teaching young children.

Contents

Trouble shooting

If you are looking for specific information and would like a head start, look at the subject areas below to see if they will be of any help:

This book caters for various age groups:

Before birth   **Babies**   **Toddlers**   **Pre-school**

Two - Five year olds

Practical, spiritual and organisational issues:

Building foundations   **Teamwork and recruitment**   **Vision**   **Family**   **Church**

Group Times   **Bible**   **Prayer**

As well as different activities and developmental needs:

Basic needs   **Bible**   **The Room**   **Music**   **Art**

Building games   **Puzzles**   **Home corner**   **Books**   **Nature**   **Play and games**

Physical   **Mental**   **Emotional and social**   **Moral and spiritual**

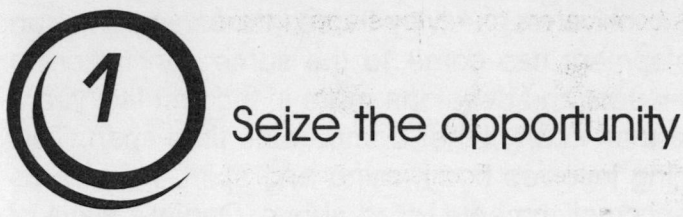

1 Seize the opportunity

"Come on, push hard, push, push. Here it comes! Keep pushing. Yes! That's it. Congratulations! You have a baby boy!"

A new life has come into the world. Without human intervention, he will die within a matter of hours. He needs someone to feed him, move him, keep him clean, dress him and regulate his temperature. In short, he is utterly helpless, entirely dependent on others.

New scene, five years later:
> *"Happy birthday dear Daniel,*
> *Happy birthday to you".*

He closes his eyes, takes a big breath and blows out all the candles on the cake. He can walk, run, skip and hop. Daniel can dress himself, feed himself, take himself to the toilet and even do most of the washing in the bath. He can communicate with others by talking, gesture and facial expression. Although he is still mainly concerned with himself, Daniel is learning to see that others have feelings and opinions that can and should affect the way he behaves. He has come a long way in five years.

Extensive research by those interested in human development has come to the same conclusion: a child learns and develops more in the first five years of life than in any other comparable time span. This learning involves body, mind and spirit. As well as the accomplishments listed above, Daniel's ways of dealing with and handling people, his feelings about himself, and his general view about what life is like are already well developed.

It seems pretty clear that those people who are responsible for Daniel would want to make the most of those first years. Surely they will want to teach him the things they believe to be most important about life. They will want to demonstrate for him a way of living that will set him on the right path as he enters school and moves towards adolescence and adulthood. If they don't, he will have to learn for himself what matters. He may copy the example of people he comes into contact with or sees on television, video or the internet. Without anyone leading him morally or philosophically, he may come to any number of conclusions that leave him dissatisfied and wondering what life is all about.

Sadly, a lack of guidance is what has been happening in our society for years. The great task of the Christian church is to reach out to young people and adults who are somehow dissatisfied, with no real clue as to why they are here or where they are going. It is our responsibility and our privelege to introduce them to the one true God who loves them and wants to have a relationship with them. Bringing them to personal faith in Jesus, then helping them to grow in that faith, is what the church is all about.

Go back to Daniel for a minute. Set a different scenario.

> What if those responsible for him taught him the truths of the Christian faith from the day he was born?

> What if he was part of a generation of children who grew up knowing and loving the Lord?

> What if he was helped to build the truth of the Bible into his life from the very beginning?

> What if, when he reached a certain age, making his own commitment to follow Jesus was the next, natural, step?

> What if he had such a grounding in the Christian faith that Bible study, prayer, lifestyle evangelism and being part of the church family were almost second nature, the obvious follow-ons to all that he already knew? What if, indeed!

Teaching children like Daniel the things of God from the very beginning is seizing a valuable opportunity that we will never again have in the same way. Communicating biblical truth in ways that are appropriate to his stage of development and understanding means that he will learn much.

So, how do we do it? Whose job is it? What exactly do we teach? These are all good questions. The rest of this book is aimed at helping you find the answers and work them out in your own situation.

Look here!

It is our responsibility and our privelege to introduce children to the one true God who loves them and wants to have a relationship with them. Proverbs 22:6

2 Whose job is it?

The Family

There was a time when this question would never have been asked. Hundreds of years ago children learned everything in the context of the home and wider family. Gradually, the place of learning extended into the community and schools; apprenticeships and formal training became the norm. The responsibility for teaching children was being shared out. In recent years, Western society has taken this to the extreme. Children may now be in nursery schools from as young as two. With both parents often in the workplace, the primary care of many children rests more with 'outsiders' than within the actual family. Consequently, many people aren't sure whose job it is to teach their children, whether it be the ABCs or how to choose right from wrong.

This dilemma has crept into the church. Because so much of a child's education happens somewhere other than the home, many parents seem to have assumed that spiritual training will also be done by others, namely the Sunday School. We ought to say at the outset that this is not a biblical conclusion. It is more a reflection of current culture.

The Bible indicates that the primary responsibility for spiritual training of children rests with the home. This pattern is clearly seen in the Old Testament. Telling and retelling the stories that explained how God dealt with his people and memorizing the laws that he gave them were essential to the passing on of the faith. Books were not a feature of everyday life, so word of mouth and example were the ways of learning. God instructed his people early on that they should observe all his commands and teach their children to do the same so that generation after generation would fear the Lord. In Deuteronomy we read this command:

 *Deuteronomy 6: 5-9*

Love the Lord your God with all your heart
and with all your soul and with all your strength.
These commandments that I give you today
are to be upon your hearts.
Impress them on your children.
Talk about them when you sit at home
and when you walk along the road,
when you lie down and when you get up.
Tie them as symbols on your hands
and bind them on your foreheads.
Write them on the door-frames
of your houses and on your gates.

Clearly it was God's intention that the passing on of the faith was to be a natural part of everyday life. Because the family was not defined as just one set of parents with their own children, the whole extended family shared the task of training the next generation. Grandparents, uncles, aunts, older siblings and cousins all joined in the care of children physically, and the nurturing of their faith.

The same command applies today. Of course, our way of life is very different from the ancient Jews but the principles that God set in place for his people then are just as valid now. We have to work them out in the context of modern life.

 ## Home and Church

This is where the home and the church work together. Whatever the make-up of the home, it is still to be the primary teacher in the things of God. A home may be defined as people who are a family by reason of birth, marriage, adoption or invitation. That covers just about every combination we see today! The Christian adults in the home, whoever they may be, take the lead in instructing the children in the faith. The church acts as the extended family, supporting them in that task.

The church can provide some spiritual input and experiences that the home cannot provide. The home is the proving ground for all that is taught, working it out in everyday life and relationships.

The responsibility is great on both sides. No matter how good a church's teaching programme is, one or two hours of input every week are unlikely to make much difference if the same principles are not upheld in the home.

In the same way, if a child is learning and growing in his knowledge of God at home, and he goes to church only to find that he is not taught or even welcomed, what will that say to him? He may come to believe that God is okay but the church is not for him. The home and the church must be in partnership. Here are some ways the church can help:

 ## Support for Struggling Parents

Very few parents today, whether Christian or not, feel confident in their task. With the general breakdown in society, and the specific breakdown in the area of marriage and family life, very few people have had good role models for parenting. They need help, and most of them know it. The church can provide help through good marriage preparation and courses in relationship building or keeping marriages strong. Support ministries, such as parent and toddler groups, play groups, courses in parenting and practical counselling for specific individuals can make a huge difference.

What about support/discussion groups for mums and dads; linking single-parent families with a mature couple in the church who can provide additional role modelling for the children; practical support such as babysitting and DIY or housework for lone parents;

older people in the church 'adopting' families with young children who have no grandparents nearby; families 'adopting' an older person whose children live far away? The needs in every community vary. Each church must discover the ways it can best support the families in its care.

 ## Spiritual Support

A church that has a strong teaching programme for under fives is not only enriching the growth of those children, it is ministering to their parents as well.

Firstly, by loving, teaching and caring for young children on Sundays, their parents are able to be in the main teaching time, focusing on what God is saying to them. For many parents, this may be their only time of interaction with the people of God in a week. For some young mums, particularly, it may be their only time 'alone' with God all week. By supporting their spiritual growth in this way we are doing them, and their children in turn, a favour.

The other means of spiritual support is in the parents knowing they are not alone. Christians are in a spiritual battle for the future of their children. Satan would love to destroy the influence of Christian homes and rob the church of its future. Standing alongside parents in passing on the faith to their children encourages them to keep going. Every parent loves to know that someone besides them cares about their child. This act of support may seem small but I believe it is very significant.

Happy Families?

In the church, as we reach out to the community, we have people from every imaginable family situation. It is important that we know relevant facts about the home situations of the children we teach. This will help us as we talk to them but also in knowing what their needs and concerns might be. If we know that a child lives with just one parent, with grandparents, or in a foster home, our conversations with them will reflect that.

Some of the children we teach may well come from homes where there is great unhappiness. They may frequently see or hear adults arguing, shouting and fighting. They may themselves be the victims of severe criticism, neglect, verbal, physical or sexual abuse. (If we suspect abuse, it may be necessary for us to notify the authorities.) We can ask God to help us understand the special needs of such children, and in the brief time we have with them, to make a difference. As we work with children who struggle in one way or another at home, we need extra love and compassion combined with godly wisdom. Knowing about their home situations enables us to pray more intelligently for them and helps us as we teach them.

Another area in which we must be sensitive is teaching about family life. As people committed to the word of God, we must somehow hold high God's ideal of one man and one woman for life, of sexual morality and purity, and of homes where children are loved, nurtured and disciplined. At the same time, we must help people to know God's love for them as individuals, however much their own situation does not reflect God's ideal. They can know his forgiveness for their mistakes, his grace to live with the consequences of their actions and his hope for blessing in the future.

As we teach under fives about families we want to help them understand that families are God's idea, that they love and care for us and that we can be helping members of our families. This is not always easy, especially with children whose families do not fit this description. They may think that God's idea of families was not a very good one! In one-on-one conversation with such children, we may be able to allow them to vent some of their anger and churned up feelings.

Working with children from disrupted or difficult family situations is a challenge. Each child's needs are unique and our approach must fit that child's personality as well as their level of understanding. As we teach under fives we need the power and insight of the Holy Spirit to demonstrate the love of God to every child, whatever the make-up of their family.

 ## Evangelism

A good teaching programme for under fives can be an aid to evangelism. Many adults will not come to church for themselves, but they will come for their children. There is still a small amount of residual sympathy for Christian things in our society. No doubt we have all heard parents say that they think it is a good idea for children to 'go to Sunday School'. I once heard someone say, "Well, I went to Sunday School and it didn't do me any harm!" Although this desire for their children to 'attend Sunday School' is often quite patronizing, we can still use it as an opportunity for God to work in their lives. They may come to church for the wrong reason but at least they will hear the right message when they get there!

The goal, then, is to develop such a good teaching programme for under fives that it draws non-Christian parents to the church for the sake of their children. This is a lofty ideal which we must keep in mind. The reality is, though, that making a first entrance to church on a Sunday is too threatening for most people. We have to use other ways of reaching them.

This is where toddler groups, parenting courses and other support ministries suggested earlier can be used evangelistically. When we have established relationships with people in these settings, we can invite them to come on Sundays. When they come to church and find that they and their children are welcomed, loved and catered for, they are far more likely to return. Teaching under fives is not directly evangelistic but it can certainly aid the evangelistic outreach of the church to young families.

Whose job is it to teach young children the things of God? It is mainly the responsibility of the home but the church acts as extended family, supporting the task of passing on the faith to the next generation. So where do we start?

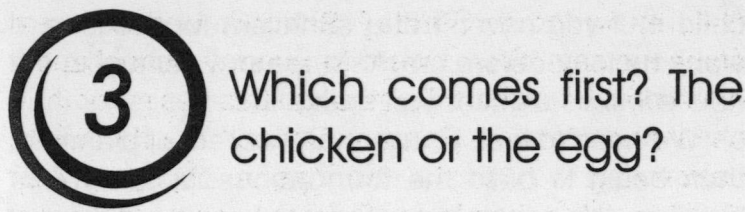

3 Which comes first? The chicken or the egg?

Pre-schoolers

It is quite likely that you are reading this book because you are already fairly convinced about teaching pre-schoolers. You may have grasped the potential of children growing up with love for God as a natural part of their lives. Or perhaps your church is awash with pre-schoolers and it has become clear that somebody has to do something —and that somebody is you! You are now desperate for suggestions. 'When are we going to get to the craft ideas?' may be your most pressing question.

Do not fear! Practical help is on the way. Before we get to it, though, we have some other work to do. When faced with the reality of a room full of toddlers every week, activity ideas can easily seem more important than theory. They may be more urgent but they are not more important.

Working effectively with pre-schoolers is not unlike building a house. Plans, foundations, bricks and mortar are all crucial. If you start with bricks and mortar, you will soon be in trouble. Without plans, there will be no direction to your work so your house may look very strange. Even if you do manage to build it, if you haven't dug sufficient foundations, it won't be long before cracks appear. Eventually, the house will be unfit for you to live in.

We need to look at one more aspect of planning, then begin to build the foundations. When you're building, this is the 'unglamorous' stage. It doesn't look very much like a house but hang in there. Once the bricks start going up, it soon takes shape.

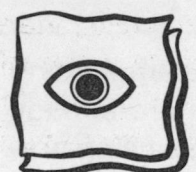 ## Vision

A very important part of planning a pre-school programme is sharing the vision and recruiting the teachers. You can't do all the teaching yourself, and if no one else is committed to the vision, you will become discouraged very quickly. So here are some pointers for communicating vision:

Know your stuff
Many of us have the tendency to see what we think is a good idea and rush headlong into trying to put it into practice without thinking if and how it would work in our particular setting.

Read this book to the end. Take time to think and pray about what God is saying for your church situation. Make some notes of your impressions and ideas, then go to a church leader. It is not necessary to have all the details of who, when and where in place but it is important to be fairly clear about what the vision is.

Start with the right person

Now you know what you are talking about, think about who you should talk to. It may be appropriate to go straight to a church leader. It may be better to 'test' your ideas on a trusted friend or a mature member of your church whose wisdom you value. Sometimes the best test of a vision is to share it with someone who at present has nothing to do with pre-schoolers.

A word to the wise from a minister's wife: don't 'recruit' a group of people who share your bias, then go to the leaders and say, "There are a number of people who feel the same way I do". This is guaranteed to put the leaders' backs up before you even start! Ask God to guide you about who you should go to first.

Choose your moment

Many a good idea in the church has never been put into practice because it was shared in the wrong place at the wrong time.

Sunday morning, after the minister has preached his heart out and 57 people are queuing to shake his hand is probably not the best time to share the idea that will solve all your church's problems! Encourage your minister or the leader you want to speak with by saying:

"I've been thinking and praying about something lately. I have some ideas to share and I'd appreciate your input. When would be a good time to chat to you about it?"

Any idea worth sharing is worth waiting for.

Work from principle to practice

This is a very good rule of thumb for any kind of change. If I present people with a list of things I think we need to be doing that involve a change from the present situation, I'm not likely to be met with wholehearted enthusiasm. But if I present some principles I believe are important, and begin to explain the vision that flows from them, people may become convinced.

If I approach any issue at the practical level of how things are going to change, people will always find a reason why we can't do it—we don't have the time, the money, the space, the manpower and so on. If, however, people change the way they view something in principle, they will do everything they can to put that principle into practice.

Many good and helpful ideas never get off the ground because people concentrate on putting the practical structure into place before they have persuaded others of the principles involved. The whole church doesn't have to be convinced before anything new can start or changes can be made but it is important to secure the commitment of key people who will be supportive during transition.

Look here!

Are you wondering about rotas and how to use them? Go to page 32!
Are you grimacing over teaching being a life sentence? Don't. Go to page 33!

Recruiting

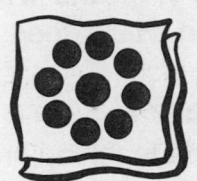

Finding the right people

Once the principle of developing a good teaching programme for pre-schoolers is established, find the people who will teach. If you have the right teacher everything else will work but if you have the wrong teacher, nothing else matters. This is an important principle to establish when you begin to recruit people to teach pre-schoolers. Many churches take care to find the right people in areas they deem to be important but just anybody can 'help out' with the 'creche'. I am indebted to my husband for caricaturing this view. In *How to Close Your Church in a Decade* (with David Cohen, Scripture Union, 1992) he cites this example of a notice given out in a church:

Please will someone volunteer to help out with the under fives; Mrs. Smith had nine children on her own last Sunday...and they all cried at the same time. It's only an hour a week and you don't need to be any good with children, just willing to be there. If three or four volunteered, then you could have a rota—so you would only have to do it once a month! (p.32)

This may be a bit of an exaggeration—but only a bit! In theory, with a commitment to the principle of good biblical teaching from the earliest years, we won't stoop to this level! In reality, finding enough of the right kind of people to work with children and teenagers is a problem for almost every church. There are no easy formulas that guarantee a fully trained, well-staffed Christian teaching programme. There are, however, questions to answer before we start looking for staff. Knowing what we're looking for and what we're asking of people is a good start. Here goes:

Who should be a teacher?

What kind of person should be teaching pre-schoolers? It goes without saying that the most important requirement is that every teacher be a committed Christian. How can we possibly communicate the love of Jesus if we do not know it for ourselves? Even very young children can sense the difference between someone who is committed to what they are doing and someone who is not. Other factors that people often wonder about are:

* **Age**

The more relevant issue is fitness. Someone must be fit and agile enough to be up and down off the floor and able to lift young children. Some people can't do this at 50. Others can still do it at 80! In terms of a lower age limit, see page 28.

* **Gender**

Traditionally, teaching under fives has been the domain of women but there are reasons why it is good to have male teachers as well:
- some children respond better to men

26

- it is good for children to see men teaching about God
- some children need a male role model
- when men teach young children it sends a strong message to the church about the shared responsibility of passing on the faith - it isn't just women's work!
- teaching pre-schoolers is a gift that God has given to some men. It is the way they can most effectively contribute to the life of the church.

*   **Experience/Professional training**
Many people feel that they need to have had some experience of working with young children in order to teach them at church. This is not necessarily so. I have known some single people with no previous experience of children to be excellent teachers. As long as a person is willing to learn, prior experience is not necessary.

Another common assumption is that the best people to teach are those who are trained teachers, nursery nurses, etc. Again, not necessarily the case.

Many people who spend their working week with young children do not wish to spend Sunday morning with them as well. Often, people who do not have daily contact with children bring a real freshness to the time on Sunday.

 ## Are there people we shouldn't ask to teach?

In these days of the Children's Act and codes of best practice, we need to be very careful about enlisting people to work with children. Your church may well have a code of practice for its youth and children's work. If this is an area you have not looked into, your denomination may be able to help you. *(The Baptist denomination has a policy called 'Safe to Grow' which helps churches take seriously the various areas of concern expressed by Social Services. Other denominations and groups have also developed programmes that can help churches think through this issue.)*

This is a big area which is being addressed by others, so we will not go into it here. Please do take it seriously, though. For reasons not at all connected with government policy there are some groups of people we need to think carefully about as we prepare to enlist teachers. Here are three groups I would prefer not to use on a weekly basis:

*   Young People
The church is not legally bound by the Children's Act unless it looks after children for more than two hours consecutively. Even so, we should honour the guidelines it contains. It is good practice not to use people under 18 as leaders of a class of children. However, many teenagers who have made clear commitments to Christ want to become involved in church life. We want to encourage them to discover their gifts and develop areas of ministry. Perhaps they can be used in groups once a month but not as the main leader. This enables them to fulfil a meaningful role without depriving them of the teaching they would get in their own age group. At this pivotal stage in their lives they need to be receivng teaching as well as the support of a Christian peer group more often

than they need to be doing the teaching.

(N.B. If a young person loses interest in church, it is tempting to give them the job of 'teaching Sunday School'. We may hope that the responsibility will keep them coming. That may be true, but just what will they be teaching, and what are we teaching them in doing this? Spiritually reluctant teenagers may be good with pre-schoolers but they will only be child minding, not passing on a living vibrant faith. We are sending them the signal that you don't have to be committed in your faith in order to teach the Bible to children. It's a difficult issue but one we need to think through carefully. If we make it a clear policy, it will be easier to handle when it is the teenager of our best friend (or even our own teenager!) in question.)

* Parents

In general I try not to use the parents of pre-schoolers as teachers on a weekly basis. *(See section on rotas)* Many churches seem to organise their 'creche rota' with the general assumption that it is the parents' responsibility to look after the children. I believe that this assumption is wrong.

While the spiritual nurture of children at home is the job of parents, the spiritual nurture of children when they are at church is the job of the people whom God has gifted in this area of ministry. In fact, if teaching pre-schoolers is also a ministry to their parents, it seems appropriate that the parents be freed from their regular responsibility with their children so that they can receive in worship or even contribute in some other way.

Many parents of young children cannot get out on

Sunday evenings (if there is a service) or to a midweek fellowship or Bible study. This makes Sunday morning all the more vital for them in terms of worship, teaching and contact with other adults.

Sometimes the people God has gifted to teach pre-schoolers do happen to be parents of young children. In this case, I would want to ensure that they are able to get out regularly to other meetings where they can worship, recieve teaching and enjoy fellowship.

(Also, most churches have the facility to record services. Teachers can then listen to the tapes during the week.)

*   New Christians

We are often guilty in the church of using the keenness and enthusiasm of new Christians in place of maturity. We can do them a real disservice by giving them too much responsibility too soon, especially when it requires them to miss the teaching and worship which they need in order to grow. Many people today are converted as adults, with no church background. They need time to get to know the Bible themselves before they try to teach it to others.

However, it is important for new Christians to realise early on that God wants them to be a contributing member of his body. They, along with teenagers and parents of young children, may be able to be used less frequently than every week. Teaching once a month, for example, would enable them to make a valuable contribution without carrying too overwhelming a responsibility. *(Again, see section on rotas.)*

How do we ask?

As you look around your church, ask God to show you who he might be calling to teach pre-schoolers. Remember, the best people are not always the most obvious.

When you have someone in mind, you can either speak to them directly or write a note. A note may often be better for two reasons: firstly, if the person is not expecting to be approached, and they have not worked with under fives recently, they are more likely to think it through carefully if they have the time and privacy to do so. If I speak to them directly, I may catch them off guard. They may be so surprised that they answer without really thinking clearly. Writing a note allows people to get over the shock in private then think and pray about how to respond.

Secondly, a note is less threatening than having someone look you in the eye. It gives people more freedom to say no if they don't think it is right for them at this time. I don't ever want someone to say yes to teaching pre-schoolers because I am standing in front of them and they feel embarrassed to say no.

If you write a note, just give a small amount of information. Give the person time to think about it and get back to you. If they are open to the idea, you can fill in the details face to face. As you chat with them in person you will be able to communicate your enthusiasm and vision and explain what the job entails. An initial note might look something like this:

You may be aware that I have responsibility for the Sunday morning teaching programme for pre-schoolers. There are a few areas where we need leaders and helpers. I wondered if this was an area of ministry that God might want to use you in. I would love to talk with you about our vision for passing on the faith to our children from the day they are born.

If you feel that this might be an area in which God can use you, please give me a ring and we'll arrange a time to chat so I can give you more details. Please be assured that agreeing to talk with me doesn't mean you have to say yes. I would just like us to explore this if you sense it may be right. If you are fairly certain this is not what God is calling you to do, feel absolutely free to say so. Either way, I would really appreciate it if you would get back to me within a week or two.

Asking people to come back to you either way helps to ensure that they do actually think about it. Also, it lets you know that they did at least get your note! Sometimes you have to chase them up but most people honour your request that they ring you. If they are not people you know well, make sure you put your phone number on the note.

 ## Regulars or rotas?

Should we have the same teachers every week or can we use a rota? The answer is yes, you can do both. The system that works best will vary from church to church, depending on how many teachers are needed and what personnel are available.

Sometimes people will be able to commit to teach every week. The continuity is good for children (and parents!). In other cases, two people 'job sharing' works well. They might alternate weeks, or do two weeks on, two weeks off. In addition, you may have people who work on a rota every third week or once a month. In the course of my work with pre-schoolers I have used every possible combination. In my church we currently have different setups in every age group—and they all seem to be working well!

No system is perfect. The security of the same teacher each week is important for children. On the other hand, it is also stimulating for them to be involved with a variety of adults. Sometimes trial and error is the only way to find out what is workable in a specific situation. We may think that the ideal is to have the same teachers every week. In reality, that may not be possible. We must assess our own situation and decide how we can best meet the needs, given the children and teachers we have.

Is teaching a life sentence?

Have you ever seen the bumper sticker that says, 'A dog isn't just for Christmas...it's for life!'? Many people feel that way about taking on responsibility in the church, particularly teaching children. They fear that if they say yes, they will be doing it until the second coming!

There was a time when people could commit to teach week in, week out, for many years. Today, those people are a rare exception. Most people find it helpful to know how long a commitment they are being asked to make. When recruiting teachers, I have found it helpful to assure people that it's not forever! I plan our teams for a school year at a time. Most church programmes operate 'normally' from September to July, then have some kind of break in August. When I ask people to teach, I generally ask them to commit for that school year. Around mid to late May I start checking with various people to see if they would like to do another year or if they need a break.

With new teachers, whether they will do every week or even just once a month, I suggest they give it a three month trial. If, after that time, they don't think it is working, (or, indeed if I don't think it is working) they can tell me and we will find someone else. That 'get-out clause' gives people the freedom to explore whether teaching pre-schoolers is their ministry. Many people have no idea about this because they have never been part of a church that had a teaching programme for such young children.

Well, the plans have been drawn and, hopefully, planning permission has been granted! Now we can start to build! Strong foundations are key to good life development. They are also crucial to the long-term success of teaching pre-schoolers. The foundations we will dig involve child development, the needs of children and understanding how they learn. So let's get started...

Look here!

Even before birth a baby can hear, respond to touch and is affected by its mother's emotional state. Turn the page and find out more about the physical, emotional and moral development of children.

5 See how they grow!

Building foundations

Building foundations for work with pre-schoolers certainly involves understanding how they grow and develop. Studies of human development have led to dozens of books on the subject, from technical textbooks to more user-friendly books aimed at expectant parents. These give details about what you can expect a baby or toddler to do at what stage. If you have only limited experience with young children, you may find it helpful to browse through a book on child development to add to your knowledge. You will learn about physical, mental and social development.

Looking at children from our viewpoint as Christians, we also need to understand a child's moral and spiritual growth alongside physical and mental development. We not only want to provide care that is appropriate for the age and stage of the child, but we want to communicate biblical truth in ways that will have the greatest impact. Secular books do not share this concern so we will look at it here.

What follows is a very brief overview of child development, with particular emphasis on moral and spiritual implications.

Before birth

In nine months a human foetus undergoes massive physical development - from one fertilized cell to a fully functioning body, capable of existing outside the protected environment of its mother's womb. But that is not the end of the story. Even before birth a baby can hear, respond to touch, and is affected by its mother's emotional state. When she is stressed, her body releases hormones that reach the baby through the placenta. The ability to hear (although the sounds are muffled by the fluid in the womb) explains why a baby responds to its mother's voice so soon after birth. The baby has been hearing it for several months!

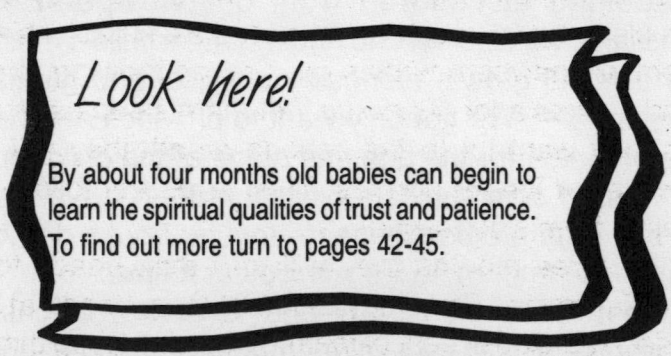

Look here!

By about four months old babies can begin to learn the spiritual qualities of trust and patience. To find out more turn to pages 42-45.

Babies

Physical

Newborn babies are completely dependent on others. They cannot feed themselves, dress themselves or even reposition themselves. In the early days of their lives, the only purposeful movement they are capable of is sucking - and that is a reflex action!

All this very quickly begins to change. Within a few weeks, their eyes will be able to focus on nearby objects. They may attempt to lift their heads to see something. You may notice a slight tightening of their muscles when they are lifted. At this stage, they may be sleeping as much as 21 out of 24 hours! This is normal - newborn babies have much growing to do, and it takes a lot of energy. Let them sleep as much as they want to! In the second month they will be awake for longer periods. Their eyes will follow an object from side to side.

By three months they will turn their heads to a familiar voice. They may also bat their hands at an object dangled in front of them. They may grasp things with their hands but they are not able to purposefully let go. They can now lift their heads when lying on their stomachs.

At four months babies will reach for objects in front of them and will turn their heads to find the source of sound. Their head and neck muscles are stronger now so you may not need to put your hand behind their heads when holding them. They will discover their fingers and become fascinated by them, although they will not realize they are part of their bodies. They will look at them, clasp them together and, of course, taste them. After this, everything starts going in their mouths. It becomes an instrument for learning and discovery.

By five months babies can hold a toy in both hands or change a toy from one hand to another. They may start to roll over and they can sit for short periods with support.

Somewhere around six to seven months they will be able to sit for a little while without support. They will also discover their feet - a nice toy which will also fit in their mouths.

At about nine months they can get on to their hands and knees and rock back and forth. They will learn to put a hand, then a knee forward, and soon they will be crawling. They may even be able to crawl up the stairs - but they won't be able to get down again. Not intentionally, anyway! Now that they can move, they can crawl to something they see or want (including things that are not toys!). They will probably enjoy standing with help. They can now use their first finger and thumb together to pick up an object.

By one year babies can pull themselves up to stand or are even able to stand alone. Then they may cry because they don't know how to sit down again. Next, they 'walk' in a sidestep, holding on to the furniture. They also use their eyes and their hands more than their mouths for exploration. They may enjoy taking things apart or emptying containers of their contents but they won't be able to put them back again.

Mental

At birth, babies do not really think, they only react but very soon their behaviour begins to have purpose. Within a few weeks they will follow an object with their eyes. They become sight and sound 'hungry', searching for things to see and hear. They respond well to colours and movement. They are entertained by having something to listen to, like music, or people talking. (But they also need times of quiet!) At this stage, if something moves out of their sight, it ceases to exist - out of sight, out of mind.

Within a few months they begin to recognize the shape of things. If an object looks like a bottle, they know it means food. Familiar sounds can be comforting, too, like the sound of mother's voice. Even the sound of approaching footsteps is a signal that someone is coming.

At five months they may turn an object around to inspect the other side of it. They think that objects in pictures are real and may reach out for them or try to pick them up. When they discover their feet, they do not yet realise that they are attached to their body. Somewhere between five and eight months the difference between mother's face and the face of a stranger becomes significant. This can cause what is often referred to as 'stranger anxiety'.

Another major mental step is the discovery of cause and effect. When they accidentally drop something from their highchair, they watch. They see and hear it hit the floor. They learn that if they let go of something, it falls and makes a noise. This is a great discovery. They do it again. Also, if they drop it, someone will pick it up. To adults, this is an annoying game. To a baby it is a significant mental milestone. They have learned that they can cause things to happen.

Another major mental step is learning that things still exist even when they cannot see them. This may happen around eight or nine months. They may cry when you take things away. Before, they forgot about it once they couldn't see it. Now they remember.

At ten to twelve months when you hold them up to look in a mirror, they will recognise you, but not themselves. If you give them a book, they will put it in the right position for reading and turn pages, usually several at a time. Their memory is developing such that they may be able to remember the next day where they put the book. They enjoy stacking things and taking apart nesting toys. They will be unable to put them back in the right order because they can't understand why the big beaker does not fit into the little one.

During the first year there is major mental development. Babies learn how to move in order to explore. This exploration is done through all the senses - seeing, hearing, tasting, touching and smelling.

♥ Emotional and social

In the first month of life a baby's emotions may seem very intense and changeable. They can be very content one minute and the next minute be crying loudly. Crying is the response for everything - hunger, pain or being uncomfortable. In the second month they may stop crying when someone holds them or even talks to them.

From very early on babies respond to people talking to them. By six to eight weeks they are smiling, then even gurgling or wriggling when spoken to. They may soon make cooing sounds, trying to talk back. By about eight months they will be making sounds like 'da-da-da' or 'ma-ma-ma'. They are imitating what they hear. It is important to speak properly to a baby instead of using baby talk all the time. They learn to speak by listening to those around them.

By about six months they are responding to parental emotions. If mother speaks crossly, they may frown. If Dad laughs, they may smile. They also recognise their own name.

'Stranger anxiety' can seem like a social setback. It is actually evidence of an emotional attachment to their parents or carers.

At twelve months they will watch adults and often try to imitate. They can understand and obey a simple command like 'wave to Daddy' or 'give it to Mummy'. They will be able to give hugs and sloppy kisses. They will probably enjoy hearing rhymes and being sung to.

✔ Moral and spiritual

A child's moral and spiritual development begins at birth. The first year of life is crucial for the development of trust. If their needs are met consistently, babies learn that they can trust. If they are not met, or if they are left to cry for extended periods, they learn not to trust. They also learn not to express their needs because they sense that no one will meet them. Trust is an inherently spiritual quality. If children learn that they can trust the adults in their lives, they will form a strong foundation for trust in God. If, however, they cannot trust the adults they can see, how will they trust the God they cannot see?

Consistently meeting the physical needs of babies helps them to feel secure and to know that they are loved. Their general view of themselves and of life is developed in this first year. When we use their names in positive and encouraging ways instead of just for correction or in anger, they are helped to feel worthwhile. When we meet their physical needs as well as their needs for affection, we help them to acquire a positive outlook. They will see life as pleasant rather than unpleasant.

By about four months babies can begin to learn patience, another spiritual quality. Because they know they can trust you to meet their needs, they can learn to wait. They know that you will feed them so they learn to wait while they see you start to prepare their bottle or food. They know what comes next.

At about eight months they can begin to learn about sharing. They hold out a toy to Mum, she takes it, then gives it back in a moment. They may cry when she actually takes it away but as she gives it back they are learning the first step of sharing - being able to let go of something, even just for a minute.

As they reach the age of 'stranger anxiety' they can be helped by not being left with complete strangers. This is why consistency in teachers at church is helpful. They are also now developing a memory. If they are left with someone different every week at church they will soon build up a store of unhappy memories about church.

It is also helpful to their development of trust that they are actually left. They learn that Mummy and Daddy leave them but that they come back. Generally the solution to stranger anxiety is not to stop leaving them but to leave them with a kiss and a 'see you soon'. They may be distressed, but they will learn that Mummy and Daddy do come back.

(N.B. I would not recommend that a parent stay with a child for a minute or two, then sneak away without the child noticing. This can appear underhanded to the child and will teach him not to turn his back in case he gets left. This will not help him in developing trust.)

We mentioned that it is important to speak properly, even to babies, because it is by hearing words used that they begin to understand their meaning. When we say to a newborn baby, 'Mummy loves you', they do not know what that means but as they hear those words frequently, spoken in a warm and gentle way and accompanied by loving and consistent meeting of their physical needs, they take on significance for them.

In the same way, we can aid their spiritual

development from their first days by letting them hear the name of Jesus used often and lovingly. As they hear that God loves them, that God made them, that Jesus loves them, they will come to understand that those words are important.

Have you ever seen a father out with a young baby for a walk? The baby is observing everything around him, and suddenly becomes excited and points to something. Dad will almost automatically look in that direction then say, 'Oh yes. Look, there's a dog. That's a dog.' Even though the child cannot yet speak, his father is helping him develop the foundations for his later vocabulary. The technical name for this is 'labelling'. We tell children the name for many things which they see and hear.

As we introduce a baby to the things we see every day, so we can just as naturally introduce him to the things of God. As Dad talks to him about the dog he can also say, 'Thank you, God, for eyes to see the dog'. Children can begin to learn about the Bible as we say to them, 'I love you. Jesus loves you, too. The Bible says that Jesus loves us'. These are the kinds of things babies need to hear at home and at church. As they approach twelve months and their memory starts to function, they will remember the things we tell them, even though they cannot yet say them themselves.

I am quite sure that this natural way of helping our children to learn about God and to know him is part of the outworking of Deuteronomy chapter six, 'Impress them [these commands] on your children' (verse 7). The problem for most of us is that we don't find it easy to speak of the things of God to one another, let alone to our children. We say, 'We were really fortunate that it didn't rain for our picnic', instead of 'Thanks, Lord, for the sunshine'. We can pray, and ask God to help us become more comfortable with our words about him. Perhaps then our children will grow up without our inhibitions, and be those who delight to speak of the things of God.

The first year of life is vital for the foundation of spiritual development. As babies have their physical needs met consistently and lovingly, they learn trust. As they hear the names of God and Jesus used in positive, affectionate and reverent ways, they realise that they are important. As they hear their own name used with love and encouragement, they form a healthy view of themselves, knowing that they are loved and valued.

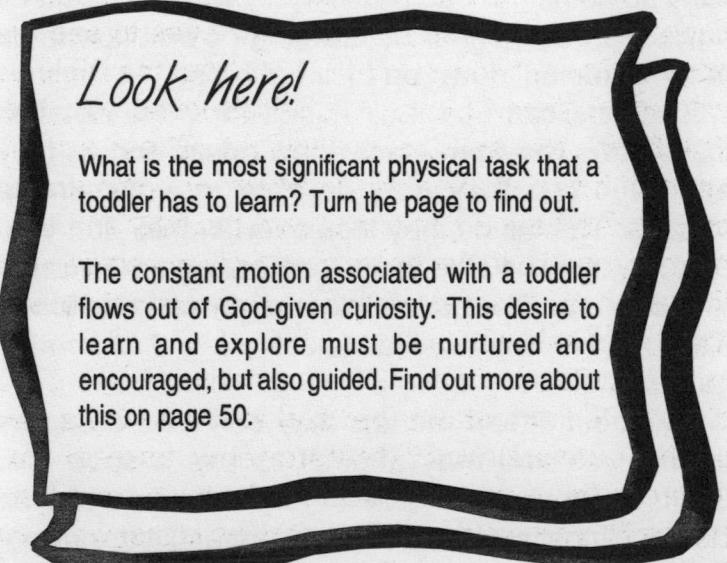

Look here!

What is the most significant physical task that a toddler has to learn? Turn the page to find out.

The constant motion associated with a toddler flows out of God-given curiosity. This desire to learn and explore must be nurtured and encouraged, but also guided. Find out more about this on page 50.

Toddlers

Physical

The most significant physical task of a toddler is learning to walk. This requires a great deal of concentration and energy. Once they have learned how, they will want to do it all the time! Soon they will be able to walk and carry something as well, then carry something in each hand. They will learn to come down the stairs either by crawling down backwards or by 'bumping' down on their bottoms.

Toddlers can use their hands for more detailed tasks now. They can stack a few bricks and as they approach two they may be able to work simple puzzles. The things they took apart in their first year they may now be able to put together again. Towards two they can hold a chunky crayon and scribble, although they may well alternate using right and left hands.

By about fifteen months they can hold a cup by themselves and may attempt to use a spoon for feeding. They will be able to take off some of their clothes (mostly at inconvenient times!) but not put them back on.

Mdπ Mental

In this second year of life mental development is linked to physical experiences. Toddlers learn by what they do. Because of this, they want to do many things. To them, the world is for exploring, for finding out what things can and cannot do. They may be fascinated by switching something on and off. They are not interested in why it works, only that it does work.

They now have mental pictures of many of the words they know. So when you say, 'drink', they know what you mean. When you say, 'Here comes Daddy', they know who you mean. As they near age two they understand most of what you say to them.

Between the first and second year, their vocabulary may increase to as many as 100 words. This may not begin to happen until after they have mastered walking - it is difficult to do two things at once! They are learning how to use language to express themselves. They may say 'book' when they want you to read to them, or 'wet' when they need to have their nappy changed. They will start putting two words together and making animal noises. They can point to various parts of their body, or to different people when named.

Although they may move rapidly from one toy to another, their attention span begins to increase. They may play alone for longer periods of time.

Emotional and social

As toddlers are learning to walk, they will have many bumps and falls. Falling doesn't hurt them nearly as much as it would hurt an adult - they don't have as far to go. Because they are not frightened they do not stiffen when they fall. They will not worry about these falls and bumps unless they see that those around them are worried. They will not be afraid to climb and explore unless they sense that those caring for them are afraid.

Toddlers will enjoy the company of an adult and enjoy sharing experiences with them. They will not yet play with other children, although they may play alongside them. They may explore other children by patting, touching or poking at them. At this age, choice of toys is not determined by sex. Boys will happily play with dolls, girls with cars and trains. Any preference for gender-related toys is probably more to do with what we make available for them to play with.

This is the age for independence. They want to do everything by themselves. They will make clear what they want to do and what they don't want to do. There are times when we can let them do those things that they can do for themselves. It often requires a great deal of patience. It is important, though, for it balances the times that we cannot let them do things for themselves.

Although they will be exploring and discovering many new things, they will also need the security of some routine. Knowing that things have a place and that they can find them in their place may help. A room that is cluttered with too many toys can be frustrating for them. They can only make limited choices. Having only some of the toys out at any given time may be more appropriate. Now that they are able to put things back together they can begin to learn to tidy up one set of toys before getting out another.

✔ Moral and spiritual

Toddlers watch adults and imitate them. They will learn much about the way to treat other people by the way they see adults behaving. They need to see an example of kindness, respect and gentleness.

In learning to exert their independence, they will begin to make choices. When should they do what they are told instead of what they want? When should they keep on making a fuss to get what they want? What can they touch and not touch? What should they do when someone hits them? They need guidance to know what is appropriate behaviour. When they make a right choice, notice and encourage them. When they choose the wrong thing, tell them why, and what would be the better thing to do. 'I asked you not to touch the video. If you touch it in the wrong place it might get broken, then we would not be able to use it. You can play with your puzzle instead.' At this age, they are often not able to work out the consequences of their actions. They will not know unless they are told, that playing with the video could break it. They do not know which items are built to withstand their child-like explorations and which are not.

They may often try to assert their will. This is part of their moral development. They need to know that there are limits and that the person caring for them is in control. Although they may be frustrated by this, it gives them security.

The constant motion associated with a toddler flows out of God-given curiosity. This desire to learn and explore must be nurtured and encouraged but also guided. Obviously, we must protect children from danger and correct wrong behaviour. But if we set too many limits, if we are always saying 'no' and stopping them doing things, we may strangle their curiosity. They may feel it is wrong to do new things, and may become increasingly dependent. I have a friend who once told me that when her daughter came asking to do something, before she said 'no', she always asked herself, 'why not?'. Often we automatically say 'no' to what a child is doing, without a good reason why they shouldn't do it. The reason is sometimes that we can't be bothered to take the time to allow them to try something new or different.

Many toddlers spend their lives being told to hurry up or walk faster. They are not dawdling on purpose. There is so much to see and hear all around them. We may have seen it all before but they haven't. Sometimes we are genuinely short of time, but often we can turn those moments into valuable spiritual input. As they gaze at all the fruits in the supermarket, we can take just a minute to say, 'Look at all the beautiful colours of fruit. I'm glad God gives us so many good things to eat.' Perhaps even we will be thrilled again with the great beauty and variety of God's good gifts to us!

Before children can learn to share, they have to understand what is theirs. At this age, if they are holding a toy or playing with it, they think it is theirs. They cannot understand that it may actually belong to someone else. Forcing them to 'share' when they do not understand about possession does not teach them to be generous. They perceive that you are making them do what they do not want to do. This is difficult, and needs to be handled gently and creatively, perhaps by offering alternative toys. When they do give a toy to another child you can thank them and encourage them. This will mean it is more likely to happen again.

The concept of sharing is outside the mental capabilities of young children. They are only just learning to see the world from their own point of view. They cannot yet see it from someone else's. When an adult asks or forces them to share their toy, it usually means that they have to give it up for someone else to play with. From their point of view this is grossly unfair. They only understand that *they* want to play with it. They cannot yet imagine that if they like it, another child might like it, too. Perhaps it is more realistic and helpful if we start by teaching them to take turns. They may play with it for a few minutes, then the other child can have a turn. In a few minutes it will be their turn again. Even this is not easy to teach. It requires patience and careful monitoring. Learning to take turns is the foundation for learning to share.

At twelve months children cannot understand about 'valuables'. They cannot appreciate that the video recorder costs more than all their toys combined. They have no idea that the china figurine on the fireplace has great sentimental value. Although they must begin to learn that there are things they cannot touch, too many 'no's' can be overwhelming. Perhaps it is best to move the most valuable or breakable items out of reach until they are older.

In the second year of life, children will want to please those to whom they have a strong attachment. In that way those people have power over them. With this power comes a responsibility to be consistent in standards of right and wrong, and to be an example that is good for them to imitate.

Look here!

If you are certain you don't have any double standards - make sure - go to page 65.
Do you know the seven basic needs of children? No? Check out chapter 6!

Two and three year olds

Physical

The third year of life is one of transition from baby to child. This can be awkward physically (and in other ways, too!). The mastery of walking means that two-year-olds want to walk down as well as up stairs. This is harder than it looks. They can climb now, too. This means they can reach all kinds of things!

Use caution with regard to medicines and cleaning solutions. They can now feed themselves fairly well and even make reasonable attempts at cleaning their own teeth. They can undo zips, poppers and maybe even buttons, although they will not be able to do them up again.

Their dexterity increases greatly. Their drawing may become more purposeful as circular movements begin to replace scribbles. Colouring within lines is beyond their physical ability. Plain paper rather than colouring books will give them more freedom.

This year they will gain control over their bladder and bowels.

π Mental

Vocabulary is constantly on the increase, and children now speak in sentences. Their brains often work faster than their mouths, so stuttering is not unusual. Grammar is a very difficult thing to learn, and this often results in statements like, 'I played with my toys and I goed to the park'. These things will sort themselves out. A child can best be helped by hearing adults speak clearly and correctly.

They are now learning about numbers and can count. That is, they can say the numbers in order. But they may not be able to correctly count how many bricks are in their tower. They are learning about sizes too and may be able to say which is bigger or smaller. They begin to have some understanding of time in relation to activities, for example, we get dressed before we eat breakfast, we go to bed when it is night. They do not yet know how long five minutes is. It might as well be a week to them!

All their thinking is related to their experiences. They can only understand things concretely. They are not capable of abstract thought. They cannot think things through by reason but only by how things look to them. If they pull down the window shade during the day, they may say, 'Look! I made it dark!'. To them, pulling down the shade makes the sun go away.

Often we try to explain things to them with our ability to use logic and link abstract thoughts. We may get frustrated when they ask the same question again. We thought we gave a satisfactory answer but we forget that they cannot think like we do and they do not know all that we know.

Two-year-olds rarely know the answer to the question 'why?'. When they have grabbed a toy from another child and we ask, 'Why did you do that?', they are not able to answer. They genuinely do not know why. Even as adults we do not always know why we do the things we do. Rather than asking, 'Why did you do this?' or 'Why were you naughty?' it might be more helpful to identify the unacceptable behaviour and explain why it is so. For example: 'You took the ball away from Sarah. She wants to play with it now so you must not take it away from her. That is not kind. You can play with the car now and in a minute you can have a turn with the ball.' They may not be impressed with your explanation but you have stopped the wrong behaviour and given them some words to help them understand. It is difficult to be consistent in this but most children eventually begin to understand.

♥ Emotional and social

In *Understanding Today's Preschoolers* an American book about under fives, the section on child development is written in the first person, from the child's point of view. This gives some very helpful insights:

I am wrongly referred to as 'terrible' just because I am negative (I say no often and emphatically) and am rebellious (I want my way). Actually, this can be viewed as a positive stage in my development. I am scaling a big hurdle in my development. I am not good at getting along with others. That's because I can't see things from their point of view. I mostly know what I want. I am just learning to take turns .

. . .I can be abrupt in changing my mind. I want what I want now. I like to give orders. I insist that I dress myself, which I can't do: but I will violently resist if you try to help. When I decide I can't, I may strike out at you for not assisting me.

My frequent change of moods may be frustrating for you. Just think what it is for me. I want, and I don't want. Making a decision is difficult for me. I am learning to have a mind and will of my own .

. . . When I am exasperating, try to be patient and remember that I am discovering who I am and what you expect of me. On the one hand, I am trying to be big and gain self-control. You expect me to conform to many behaviours which you consider appropriate. A few months ago I didn't even know I was a person. To become a person in my own right, I sometimes disagree with or defy you. I am trying to establish my preferences. Sometimes you disagree with my preferences of behaviour. Do I do what my parents want me to do? Do I do what I want to do? It seems I can't do both at the same time .

. . . If I am to rely on myself and feel capable of doing the tasks before me, I must be given the right to choose. I must also learn some limits. I get many commands. I have a difficult time learning rules. To remember a rule, I have to think about too many things at one time - when and where and under what conditions I can and cannot do.

I know that you expect me to gain bowel and bladder control. How you assist me in this affects my feelings about myself and your power. Shaming me for an 'accident' is a way of using your power over someone smaller. Shaming me for what I cannot help

*or don't know how to do may cause me to be deceitful.
I may even hide to do it. Shaming me causes me to
doubt my worth. Accept my efforts to gain control,
and I will feel worthwhile .*

*. . . The way I get along with others and how I
behave to get what I want are well established by
age three. These patterns of behaviour are difficult
to change.* (Waldrop, C. Sybil, *Understanding Today's
Preschoolers* (Convention Press, 1982), pp. 30-31.)

In this passage the child mentions not being good
at getting along with others because he can't see
things from their point of view. This is often confused
with selfishness. Young children are self-centred, as
opposed to selfish. Self-centred is only viewing things
from one perspective - my own! Selfish is when I can
see someone else's point of view but I choose mine
anyway. I know how others feel or what they want
but I am more interested in me.

Two year olds do not yet have the necessary
mental processes to understand how another person
feels. They cannot put themselves in their place. So
when they are asked, 'How do you think Mark feels
when you hit him?', they cannot answer because they
honestly do not know. It hurts when someone hits
them, but they do not realise that it must hurt others
when they hit them. We must assist children in
learning to see things from another's point of view.
Rather than asking the above question, it might be
more helpful to say, 'Please don't hit Mark. It hurts
him when you do that and makes him sad'. As they
get a bit older they can also be helped to understand
if they are told, 'You do not like it if Mark hits you. He
does not want you to hit him either'.

Young children are often accused of being selfish when they are actually only being self-centred. They are not choosing their own wishes above the wishes of others. They only know what they want and are not yet aware that others have preferences too.

The last paragraph of the quote concerns relationships with others. This is a crucial time for social development. At this age, patterns of relating to other people are becoming firmly established and will be difficult to alter. If children get what they want by throwing tantrums or by whining, they will learn to manipulate people to get their own way.

I well remember one of my own children telling me, 'If you don't let me do what I want I will be naughty and horrible'. I quickly assured her that this approach would not get her very far and that she was more likely to get what she wanted by behaving nicely!

Children soon learn whether crying, making a scene or throwing a tantrum will get them what they want. If it does, they develop a pattern of controlling others by manipulation.

We have already said that children are imitators of the adults in their lives. If they see us manipulating others to get what we want, they will learn to do the same. If, on the other hand, they see us treat them and others with respect, they will learn to respect the wants and needs of others.

Moral and spiritual

The child is beginning to develop a conscience, not motivated by an internal conviction of right and wrong, but determined by external factors. What adults allow is right, what they don't allow is wrong. Thus, consistency is important in this first stage of conscience development. If throwing bricks around is allowed one day and not allowed the next, they become confused. If hitting some people is okay but hitting others is not okay, they are unable to know which is which.

Important foundations are laid for forgiveness and unconditional love. It is not helpful for a young child to hear an adult say, 'I'm not talking to you because you were naughty', or, 'I won't give you a hug right now because you have been horrible'. They need to know that you always love them, even when you do not like what they are doing. Isn't it good that God doesn't stop talking to us just because we have been horrible!

Often children of this age say or do things which entertain and amuse others. 'Party pieces' are fun from time to time but we need to be careful that children do not interpret that they are loved or accepted more when they 'perform'. As they become aware that you always love them, they can also begin to be aware that God always loves them.

In the third year children begin to understand the concept of family. They have an awe and wonder at creation. They will be able to know some things about Jesus; that he was born, that he grew up, that he was part of a family. They begin to understand that Jesus loves people and wants people to love and help each other.

Affirming their attempts to be kind or helpful will encourage a positive self-image. It will also encourage further attempts!

Three and four year olds

Physical

Development of the larger muscles means that three year olds can jump, walk on their toes, use a climbing frame, throw a ball and ride a tricycle. At age four they can hop on one foot, skip, somersault and kick a ball with some accuracy.

Small muscles are developing too. They may be able to draw a person now or at least a head and face. As they approach four they may draw arms and legs as well but probably no body! They will begin to use scissors, and can manage well with pencils and ordinary crayons as opposed to chunky ones. Four year olds may be able to write their own name or at least form some of the letters.

At three they can usually manage by themselves in the toilet, although some dungarees and belts can be a bit tricky! As the months go by, four year olds will learn to dress themselves and put on their own shoes. You will still need to tie them for them. At this age velcro fastenings give a great deal of independence!

Mental

Vocabulary is ever on the increase and three year olds will talk freely, both to themselves and others. They can remember rhymes well now and enjoy singing. They have many mental images associated with words or experiences. This enables them to pretend in play - either in role play or in pretending actions.

Three and four year olds are very inquisitive. They are often asking why or how. This is their God-given curiosity at work again. Much patience is required to answer their questions in ways they can understand.

Four year olds are often highly imaginative. They may spin great tales of flight and fancy. Sometimes they find it difficult to distinguish fact from fantasy. They may genuinely believe the stories they hear about fairies and dragons. Thus, when a four year old tells you he has just seen a fairy queen in the back garden, he is not deliberately lying. He is trying to work out what is fantasy and what is reality.

At four, children are still not able to think logically. They cannot combine several thoughts to reach a conclusion. They are literalists - they think concretely and cannot understand the abstract meaning of words. When they hear an adult saying, 'He is a barrel of laughs', they are wondering how you put laughs into a wooden container.

Sarcasm is beyond a young child as well. I remember when Samuel, my youngest child, spilled his drink at teatime. It went all over the table and dripped onto the floor. I said, 'Thanks a lot, Sam!' Cara, who was just five, said 'Mummy, why did you say thank you to Samuel? You didn't really want him to spill his drink did you?'

At this age, language exceeds thinking. That is, children can talk about things they do not understand. And talk they do! If no one happens to be around they will chatter on to themselves, using words they have heard without having any idea what they mean.

This ability to remember and repeat things without understanding has serious implications with regard to spiritual things. We will look at this in more detail later, but for now it is sufficient to say that children are capable of memorising large amounts of words, including Bible verses, without having any idea of what they are saying. We often think children understand more than they do because of their large vocabulary.

Emotional and social

Three year olds are now ready to play *with* other children rather than alongside them. They are beginning to understand what belongs to whom and may be able to take turns. Sharing is still very difficult. If children perceive that something is theirs, they will struggle to understand why they have to let someone else play with it.

They are able to discern emotion by facial expression and tone of voice. They know whether their parents are pleased or displeased with them or with a situation. At four they may start to express their own emotions - 'I am happy' or 'I feel sad'.

Four year olds imitate adults in actions and attitudes. They may be fascinated with the jobs they see adults doing, particularly if those jobs involve uniforms, such as firemen, nurses, postmen or train drivers. They may pretend to talk on the telephone or type. They may pretend to use a hammer and saw or do the cooking. It is always interesting to watch children when they are imitating you. Many is the time Steve and I observed our own children 'playing' church. One would announce the songs and 'read' the Bible and the other would preach the sermon! It is often very sobering to hear our children speaking to each other in the same way that we speak to them. They learn a lot, positively or negatively, from the way they see us treat them and others.

At four children can do many things for themselves. They can also begin to do things for other people. They can do things that are helpful at home. They can help look after a younger child. They can help another child with a difficult puzzle or toy. They are also developing a sense of humour and can have a real sense of fun with adults.

Moral and spiritual

Three or four year olds think that their parents, or any adults who have responsibility for them, are infallible. They will believe without question what they are told. The rules adults make are law to them. When one child sees another doing something he is not allowed to do he may say, 'You are not supposed to do that'. When asked why, he may say, 'Because my dad says so'. At this stage of their moral development children will obey the rules, not from an inner desire to do the right thing but, in order to avoid punishment. Their moral behaviour is limited by their thinking. As their mental processes develop they will be able to understand that they can do things for others and others can do things for them.

Another quote from *Understanding Today's Preschoolers* helps us understand the moral development of three- and four-year-olds:

I judge the goodness or badness of an action by the damage done. I think it is worse to break four glasses while helping my mother set the table than to break one glass while reaching for a forbidden cookie.

I judge the badness of an action by the severity of the punishment. If you only say, 'Now, dear, stop doing that' when I am demolishing the flower arrangement on a neighbour's table, then that is not quite as bad as my taking a flower from a vase at home for which you slap my hand.

To me, what you stop, condemn, or punish, is wrong and what you approve, accept, or reward is right.

This is the way my conscience develops. You stop my annoying and hurtful behaviour, and an inner voice warns me when I disobey the rules you have taught. When you laugh at what I do or give acceptance to what I do, I feel okay about continuing those behaviours. My conscience says: 'Go ahead. This is not against the rules'.(Waldrop, C. Sybil, *Understanding Today's Preschoolers*, p. 40.)

Children's willingness to accept what adults tell them is significant in terms of their spiritual development. They will believe what they are told about God. This is wonderfully positive because they can understand so many foundational truths now - God made the world, God made people, Jesus loves me, the Bible tells us how God wants us to live, and so on. But they will also believe and remember negative things they hear about God. If they hear God's name used as an expletive, or if they are threatened with 'God will get you for that', they are not helped in their understanding of God's true character.

Children may not remember many facts and details of the Bible stories they hear, but they detect atmosphere and develop attitudes which will be hard to change later. We must use concrete, specific words that they can understand. If we use abstract or figurative language they will distort the meaning because the mental pictures they have for the words we are using are literal, not symbolic. If we talk about Jesus as the bread of life or the light of the world they will think literally of a loaf of bread and a lamp. They cannot understand these images yet.

Double standards

As we think through the implications of a child's moral and spiritual development there are two points I would like to make.

Firstly; we need to think carefully about how we sometimes have one standard for a child and another for ourselves. We do not allow a child to take toys from someone else and we explain about taking turns and being kind. Yet when it is time to leave we may snatch a toy away from a child saying, 'Put that away now', without any explanation or warning. You can imagine how this appears to them. You understand that these are two different situations but they do not. To them it appears that they are not allowed to take things from people but you are.

With their limited capacity for reason and logic they cannot work this out by themselves. Even after a simple explanation they may not understand completely but they will know, at least, that you have tried to help them understand. The very nature of the fact that adults are responsible for children means that there will be times when they have to abide by what we say, even when they don't understand. If we do our best to be consistent and provide explanations when we can, it enables them to trust us more easily in the other times.

Secondly; as you read this section on child development perhaps you learned more about how young children act, and why. This will affect the way you respond to them and interact with them. You may, however, have read some of the examples of things you might say to children and be thinking, 'This is all very well but it sounds a bit too unreal, too nicey-nice. You don't know the children I have to deal with'. That is true. I don't know those children. But I do know my own children and the children I teach. So I know that sometimes, at the end of a busy day or when I am tired, or when the children are particularly exasperating, I don't always respond in the best way with a smile on my face. I know that sometimes, in the heat of the moment, all my good intentions fly out the window. Many is the time that I have come away from an incident on a Sunday morning, or with my own children, and I know that I have not handled it well or responded in a right and godly way. All of this is easier to write on paper than to put into practice.

But I believe it is important to learn as much as we can about children and have some guidelines for the most helpful ways to deal with them. At least then we have something to work towards, a general direction in which to head. Of course we will fail at times but I would rather try and fail than have no standard at all. It may hurt to get it wrong sometimes but without a standard you don't have the joy or satisfaction of ever knowing you got it right or succeeded.

I am thankful that I am loved by a God who knows that I won't always get it right. He knows my weaknesses and my failings. He does not stand over me with a stick to beat me every time I am less than the best. Rather, he stands over me in love, ready to forgive, and give me his power to go on.

He has given me clear guidelines for what is right and wrong. He is patient with me and encourages me as I move on to the ultimate goal of becoming more like Jesus. And so I endeavour to do the same for the children in my care, whether they are my own or my responsibility through teaching or child care. Knowing from the outset that I will not be perfect and that I will make mistakes actually gives me greater freedom. I am willing to try because I am not afraid of failing. With God I know there is always forgiveness and a new start.

So, be careful, and be encouraged. Be careful about consistent standards and appropriate explanations. Be encouraged that you do not have to be perfect - only willing to learn.

! The first five years of a child's life are very busy indeed! They come into the world equipped with only their functioning human body and their unique genetic makeup, a combination of traits from their mother and father. As parents, teachers and care-givers we have the opportunity to influence them in terms of environment, relationships, intellectual stimulation, experiences and spiritual life. This is both an exciting and awesome responsibility. How we need God's help to adequately take up the challenge!

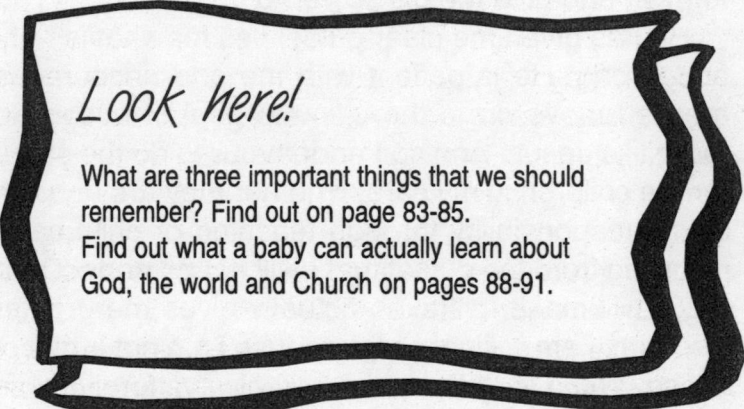

Look here!

What are three important things that we should remember? Find out on page 83-85.
Find out what a baby can actually learn about God, the world and Church on pages 88-91.

See how they learn

Seven basic needs

Many years ago we built an extension on the house we were living in. I remember looking out the window every day for several weeks and being disappointed. How could the builders have worked all day and there still be nothing that looked remotely like a new kitchen to show for it? They told me to be patient; "Once we get started on the walls it will go very quickly, you'll see." Funnily enough, they were right. And when my beautiful new kitchen was finished, it was worth the wait. Although I didn't often say to myself, "I sure am glad they took time to dig good foundations for this", I am quite certain that I would not have enjoyed the kitchen so much if it had been plagued with the problems that come from inadequate foundations.

You've read a lot of pages already and not one craft idea yet! Be patient: once we get to the practical nuts and bolts, you'll see things take shape. In the long run, your work with pre-schoolers will be more effective for hanging in there at this foundation stage.

We've already established that children learn an incredible amount in the first few years of life. How do they do it? They certainly don't read books or go to seminars! In fact, they learn in ways that fit their level of understanding, not through techniques so much as through attitudes and atmosphere. Children learn first of all by having their needs met. We've looked at the importance of meeting physical needs to build a basis for trust. As physical needs are taken care of, children are free to learn through their emotional/mental/social needs. Let's look at some of these basic needs:

1 Love

Most psychologists would agree that love is a child's first need. One of the greatest things any person can have is the knowledge that someone loves them. Designer toys and clothes matter little next to unconditional love. This may be one of the greatest unmet needs in today's children. In Western society parents are generally able to buy their children more things, but what the human spirit cries out for is love. To a baby, love is being fed, being kept warm, clean and dry, being cuddled when fretful, and being allowed to sleep when tired. As children grow, love is taking time to play with them, to listen to them, to answer their many questions. It is providing them with activities suitable for their stage of development. Love is giving them guidelines, but also allowing them some reasonable choices. Love is one of the greatest gifts adults can give to children. Being loved provides the foundation for them to respect themselves, to learn to love others and to understand and accept God's love. As we work with under fives we can ask God to give us his love for each child in our care.

② Acceptance

Children need to know that their parents and other adults accept them for who they are. Acceptance is closely linked with love. We must accept children all the time, even when we disapprove of their behaviour. Acceptance of a child doesn't mean we never correct them but it involves them knowing that they are accepted for who they are, not for the things they do. If they feel they have to earn acceptance, it may result in undue submissiveness or in rebellious and outlandish behaviour in an attempt to attract attention. Knowing that they are always accepted by God is a very powerful thing as children come to understand that God loves them and accepts them just as they are.

③ Security

Children need to feel safe physically and emotionally. They will feel safe in an environment where there are some controls and limits. They need an adult to set boundaries to protect them from others and from their own lack of control. When children feel secure they are more able to cooperate with and think of others. If they do not feel safe, they must expend energy trying to meet their needs for security.

Children find emotional security in relationships with parents and other adults. We want our children to have the best. So often we express this by giving them things when what they really need is us. As Christians we know that there is no real security in material things. As we model Christ-like relationships with children, we help them learn to find security in God his kingdom.

④ Trust

As children learn to trust the adults who care for them, foundations are laid that will enable them to trust in God. We have already looked at how infants develop trust through the prompt and consistent meeting of their physical needs. As children grow we can continue the building of that trust through our ongoing relationships with them. We listen to what they want to say to us, we help them find solutions to their problems, we correctly answer their questions and we do what we say we will do. We keep the secrets they tell us and we don't gleefully report their 'funny' mistakes for the entertainment of other adults. All these things help them to know they can trust us.

⑤ Self-respect

The way children see themselves depends on their experience of love, acceptance, security and trust. Children who have known all these things will develop self-confidence. Children who feel rejected and unloved will see themselves as unworthy and of little value. They may tend to act out what they sense those around them expect them to be.

By the age of three, children have a good idea of what the adults in their lives expect of them. If adults expect them to be naughty, children will probably live up to those expectations! If they are treated with respect and know they are loved, they will learn to respect themselves and treat others in the same way.

Loving and respecting children does not mean we

overlook their wrong behaviour. However, children are more likely to attempt to change these wrong behaviours in an environment where their efforts are met with positive affirmations and acceptance.

(6) Dependence and Independence

Children need a certain degree of independence. They need to know that there are some things they can do for themselves because they have reached that stage in their development. On the other hand, they need to know that there is an adult around who can help them when they are unable to do something. This is not always an easy balance to achieve!

Sometimes we have to let children start something by themselves, but be ready to assist them when they are not able to complete the task. It is important for their development of independence that we let them try, even if we think they may fail. Children who are overprotected often become fearful and anxious about trying anything new.

We need to create an atmosphere in which children know that they will be allowed to do that which they are able to do, but will be restrained from dangerous or destructive behaviour. Also, they will receive adult assistance when they need it without hearing, "I told you you wouldn't be able to do it yourself"!

(7) Discipline and Guidance

We have already said that children feel safe in an environment where there are some controls and limits. They often test these limits but they need to find that the limits are enforced. Children who are used to no control may appear to be full of bravado and even defiant. In reality, they are often full of fears and very insecure.

Despite the evidence that children need discipline, it has received a lot of bad press in recent years. Anyone who advocates discipline may be regarded with scepticism or even scorn. Discipline is often mistakenly associated with harsh punishment and tyrannical dictatorship! There is a general lack of understanding about what discipline actually is. True discipline implies learning. The root word, 'disciple' means a follower, one who is learning from someone else. It implies a process of gaining knowledge and understanding. As an adult disciplines a child, the child learns (sometimes after many attempts!) to be responsible for his own behaviour. The ultimate goal is that the discipline will come from within; it will result from self-control rather than external enforcement.

Children are not born with self-discipline or the ability to control their own actions. It is the responsibility of their parents and other significant adults in their lives to set limits and controls that are maintained with love, consistency, clarity and patience. In this kind of relationship, a child can learn self-control.

In addition to discipline a child needs guidance in knowing how to be safe, in learning to relate to other people and in developing various skills. Many people make the mistake of thinking that it is better to let them figure it all out for themselves, a kind of trial and error. Too frequently it ends up being mostly error!

Children look to adults for guidance. Where it is not given overtly, they have to pick up clues from adult behaviour. As they try to put together the clues to how to develop in all these ways, effective ways of relating to people often remain a mystery.

It is important that we as Christians redeem discipline and guidance from the rubbish heap where they have been tossed. Loving discipline and godly guidance are critical for the best development of our own children and those we teach.

Young children are constantly learning. Everything around them teaches them something. If we meet their needs, they learn positive things about life and the world around them. If we don't meet their needs, they still learn but what they learn does not help them develop into well-adjusted, healthily functioning children. As we seek to meet the basic needs as just outlined, it is good to be aware of some of the ways in which young children learn. Here are a few:

Seven ways they learn

1 Relationships

Through relationships with adults and others, children acquire facts and information but they also learn feelings and attitudes. To a young child actions and attitudes speak far louder than words. Children may hear the words 'share' and 'be nice', but if they do not see these words being acted out towards them and others, they will learn their own ways of dealing with people from the attitudes they have seen demonstrated rather than the words they have heard spoken.

In the same way, a child who hears the words 'I love you' accompanied by gentle affection, a warm smile and a kind voice, learns about appropriate ways to express love.

Children learn a lot about themselves through relationships. They sense whether they are loved, valued and respected. A significant part of their self-image is determined by relationships rather than words. A teacher who is able to say all the right words, but not able to develop warm and caring relationships with children is not helpful. A teacher who conveys interest through facial expression, time spent with children and attention to their needs is far more effective. Sometimes the most important learning takes place when no one is aware of it and without a word being spoken.

Children also learn attitudes through relationships. A young child does not naturally fear or dislike a child from a different racial or ethnic group. That attitude is learned from others. Children will not consistently manipulate others to meet their own needs unless someone has demonstrated to them that using others is an effective means of getting what they want.

Children learn far more than we realise through relationships. Feelings and attitudes about themselves and others are more often 'caught' than 'taught'.

(2) Physical senses

All that we learn is taken in through one of our five senses. For a newborn baby, touch may be the most significant of the senses. As hearing develops they learn to distinguish one voice from another, and pleasant sounds from unpleasant. As vision becomes clearer they recognise familiar faces and objects. Even taste and smell are important early on. They know the smell of their mother and of milk or formula. They taste the milk and as solid food is introduced they respond to new and exciting tastes.

Children learn much about the world around them through their senses. They learn about hard and soft, hot and cold, safe and unsafe through touching. They learn about objects by seeing them, touching them, and even tasting them. A child can learn much by smelling different foods or flowers. As children hear different sounds, they learn to recognise them and distinguish where they are coming from. Most children enjoy listening to music. We can help children learn by stimulating and developing their senses.

(3) Imitating

Children imitate what they see and hear others doing. They watch others use knives, forks and spoons and they learn how to feed themselves. They hear others speaking and they learn to talk. If they see others hitting and acting violently, they will imitate that as well. If they hear shouting, harshness and rude language they will copy it. Children imitate as a means of learning. They also imitate as a means of play. Children may pretend to talk on the telephone, wash dishes, drive a car or play a sport. Which parent has not laughed one minute and cringed the next as they see or hear their children imitating them?

Children learn a lot by imitating. Unfortunately, in their first few years they do not have the ability to distinguish between those things it is good to imitate and those things they should not copy. As parents and teachers we need to be careful to give them something good and positive to imitate.

 Curiosity

Children are born curious! Even very young babies turn their heads to see and hear what is going on around them. As they grow, they examine everything in sight by touching, tasting, shaking, hitting or even throwing it!

As they learn to talk they may ask many questions. Why does it make that noise? What is this for? Sometimes it is difficult to be patient in answering so many questions. Other times we may not know the answer to the questions. Why is it raining when I want to play in the garden? Which is nearer - heaven or space? Most adults don't like to admit they don't know the answer but a child is helped more by our honesty than a made-up, incorrect answer. Providing toys and activities that arouse and stimulate their God-given curiosity helps children learn.

Answering children's questions can often prove difficult and time consuming. It is important, though, because it helps them to know we are interested in them and encourages them to continue to be motivated by curiosity. We should always be truthful (even when that means saying, 'I don't know the answer to that question'), give accurate answers and keep the explanations at a level the child can understand.

We also need to make sure we know just what it is the child is asking so that we answer what they want to know.

Once a young child came and asked his father, 'Dad, where did I come from?' His father had been dreading this inevitable day, so he drew a deep breath and then gave his son a detailed explanation about the facts of life. Afterwards he asked, 'Son, what made you ask that question?' The boy shrugged and replied, 'Well, the new girl next door says she comes from Yorkshire and I just wondered where I came from?'

Curiosity is healthy and it is the beginning of discovery. Children learn as we encourage their natural urge to explore and ask questions.

 **Repetition**

Learning requires memory and memory needs developing. That is why repetition plays such an important role in learning for the young children. Read it again! Sing it again! Do it again! Often we tire of it - but they don't! As they hear a song over and over again, they learn the words. As they work a puzzle many times, they learn how the pieces fit together.

When I taught one to two year olds on Sunday mornings each week I would sing different songs that developed the teaching theme for that day but each week I also did the same simple finger play two or three times. The first week they just watched me in amazement. Then, after four or five weeks, the older ones could do it themselves. They learned through repetition. Even with three to five year olds I find that if there is time at the end of Group Time and I ask them what they want to sing, they always choose the same songs.

Children acquire new skills through repetition. A toddler cannot drink from a cup without spilling the first time he tries. He must do it over and over again to get it right. He needs to be encouraged in his attempts to master new tasks.

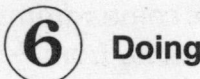 **Doing**

Children learn best through firsthand experiences. They learn by doing. We can talk to a child about Spring. We can look at pictures and books but a very young child learns the most about Spring as we point out the daffodils pushing their way up through the soil, as we notice buds on trees and bushes and as we listen for the birds singing in the morning.

Children enjoy doing things for themselves. We need to plan activities that they can do. If an art activity is so difficult that we have to do the work for them, then they will not learn. They have a sense of satisfaction in what they can accomplish themselves. If we provide an activity that has to be glued, folded or coloured in a certain way in order to turn out 'right', children may feel that they cannot produce something that is acceptable unless it is just like the one the teacher made.

With under fives, the fun and the learning in most activities is in the doing, not in the finished product. So if a three year old is painting, it does not matter what it looks like. The important thing is that they did it themselves and that someone encouraged their efforts.

When a young child is gluing, they may need help spreading the glue but they can stick the picture on the paper themselves. It doesn't matter to them if it is upside down or crooked, unless they have heard an adult tell them they must put it on in a certain way.

Providing 'doing' activities for under fives is important. This can prove very time-consuming in the home for parents and other carers but it is a vital part of their learning. At church, teachers can provide activities that enable children to learn through doing and to derive satisfaction from their growing independence.

 Play

Play is work to children. It is their natural way of learning. When they play they can practise new skills, experiment with many different materials, discover, pretend, and create. As they play with others they learn social skills, how to relate to others, how to take turns and share and how to solve problems. Because play is their natural activity it provides countless opportunities for conveying spiritual truth and teaching biblical principles.

If a casual observer were to walk into any class of under fives in our church they might say, 'They are only playing'. They *are* playing but as they play we are teaching them the things of God. We may tell them the Bible says 'Be kind'. As two children take turns with the same toy they are learning how to relate this Bible truth to life. We may tell children how to behave. Play gives them the opportunity to practise what we have said.

Understanding that under fives learn through relationships, the physical senses, imitating, curiosity, repetition, doing and play helps us to provide activities that maximise the time we have with them at church. Developing a relationship with each child we teach, stimulating the physical senses and being an example worth imitating all help children learn the right things. Encouraging their curiosity, providing many of the same activities, songs and stories again and again and letting them do what they can for themselves helps us to teach effectively. Guiding 'hands-on', here and now experiences through play enables us to show them how to apply the truths of God's word to their lives.

Children can learn in many ways. Wise teachers try to make the best use of all of them.

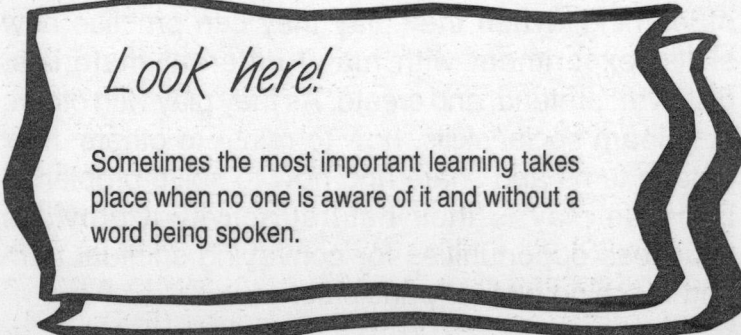

Look here!

Sometimes the most important learning takes place when no one is aware of it and without a word being spoken.

Three important things to remember!

 Abstract concepts are out; concrete, literal, here and now is in

Young children do not have the mental ability to understand the abstract. Their knowledge and experience is limited enough that they can only deal with what they have some experience of. As adults, we know about enough things that even if someone describes something we haven't experienced, we can put together some mental picture of it from the things we do know. Young children cannot do this.

The biggest implication of this for the teaching of spiritual truth is in terms of symbolism. Much of our understanding of the Bible is based on being able to think symbolically and abstractly. It is a rare pre-school child who can do this. We must teach them stories from the Bible that are about things they have some experience of. In the next section we will list some of those things that they can begin to understand but let me illustrate here by an example of some things they cannot understand.

Many of Jesus' parables make great stories but they are symbolic of spiritual truth. The story of the woman who lost a gold coin or the shepherd who went looking for one lost sheep are interesting for little children. It is highly unlikely, though, that they can make the connection between the story and the concept that heaven rejoices when a sinner repents! So why not tell them a story about something they can understand, like Elisha's friends who made a room for him to stay in at their house (II Kings 4).

83

They know about houses, friends and a place to sleep. They can begin to see that this was a way of being kind. (The one parable of Jesus that is an exception has to do with kindness. It is the story of the kind man, otherwise known as the good Samaritan. The more subtle issues in this story, like racism and stuffy religiosity are better left for when the children are older! You can use the main facts, though, and begin the story by saying, "One time Jesus told the people a story about a man who...")

The story of David and Goliath is very popular. What do we usually teach from it? No matter how small or insignificant you are, God can still use you. This is a great spiritual truth but it is a big jump from stories about scary giants, slings (what's that to a modern child anyway?) and killing people, to understanding that God can use me. Are you getting the drift? Stick with literal and concrete things.

② Knowledge is built by repetition

We have already said that repetition is one way children learn. The implication for our teaching is that basic spiritual truth needs to be repeated many times. It is okay to use the same Bible stories more than once. It is probably better not to use the same story on four consecutive weeks but you could certainly use a curriculum for a year, then repeat it the next year. The children will be a year older and they will take in a bit more of the story as well as what we are teaching through it each time.

③ Vocabulary exceeds understanding

Once children learn to talk they can be taught to say almost anything. Children usually have an amazing capacity for memorisation. They can be taught to quote Shakespeare but that does not mean that they understand it at all. The implication for us is that we must not simply teach children to repeat what we have said, either in stories or Bible verses. We must do our best to make sure that they understand. Three year olds can learn a 'memory verse' every week. That is great, but we must make sure they know what it means and how it relates to their lives. Otherwise, what they might grow up believing is that the Bible is for memorising to gain someone's approval or win a prize. What we want them to know is that the Bible is for obeying and that it has to do with their lives every day.

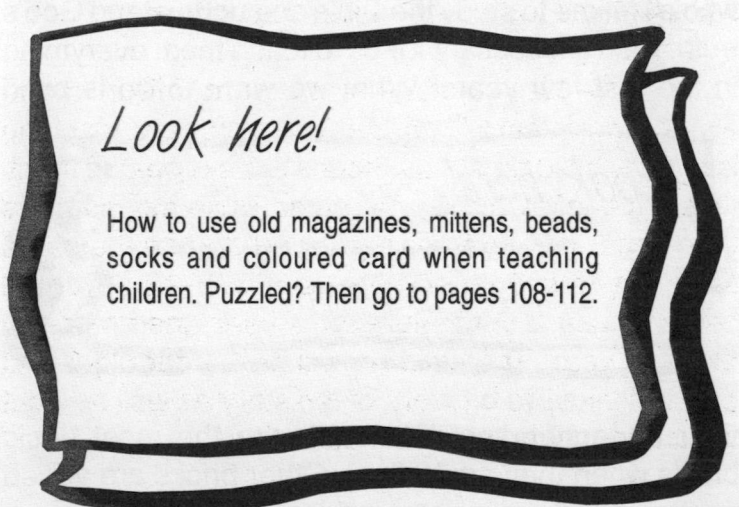

Look here!

How to use old magazines, mittens, beads, socks and coloured card when teaching children. Puzzled? Then go to pages 108-112.

7 What can they learn?

The Bible, God, the world...

The Bible is an enormous book. There is so much in it that it can be hard to know where to start in understanding and obeying it. If this is true for us as adults, how much more so as we begin to teach God's word to young children. We can be helped if we remember that we are talking about building foundations in their lives. Our goal is that they will grow up knowing Jesus; they will have a whole lifetime to study the Bible and understand God's truth. It isn't necessary for us to teach them everything in the first few years! What we want to do is build

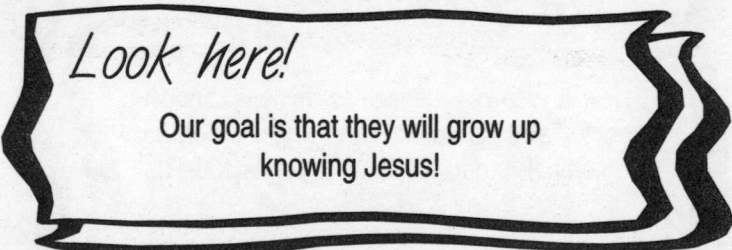

Look here!

Our goal is that they will grow up knowing Jesus!

their understanding. We start with the most basic bricks when they are babies. Other bricks are added as their ability to understand increases.

What are the basic bricks? What kinds of things can and should children learn? There may be many answers to these questions but let's look at what they can learn in eight different areas. These are not exhaustive, though they do cover a huge breadth of biblical principles. In each area we will start with the most basic statements and progress in how children can understand.

The rate at which children can comprehend these truths will vary; some children will learn faster than others. Just as with the developmental tasks we looked at previously, it is not so much the pace but the consistent progress that matters.

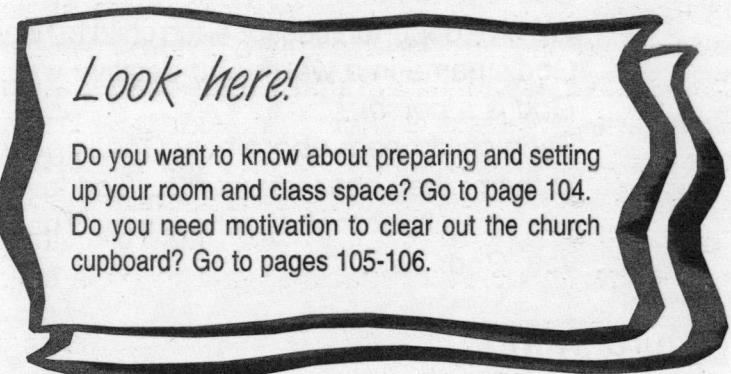

Look here!

Do you want to know about preparing and setting up your room and class space? Go to page 104. Do you need motivation to clear out the church cupboard? Go to pages 105-106.

Babies and toddlers

God

Babies and toddlers can learn that:
God is a name.
We give opportunities for each child to hear God's name in a warm and positive way.
God is a person.
Each child hears about how God is good to them; they hear the words, 'God loves you'; they hear their teachers say, 'Thank you, God...'

Natural world

Babies and toddlers learn that:
God made things that we can see, touch, taste, smell and hear.
We give opportunities for children to explore and discover what God made.
God made the animals.
Each child sees pictures of animals and hears that God made the animals.

Jesus

Babies and toddlers can begin to understand that:

Jesus is a name.
We provide opportunities for each child to hear the name of Jesus used warmly and positively.

Jesus is a person.
Each child sees picture story books and hears stories about Jesus as a baby, child and man; they hear the words, 'Jesus loves you'; they have a growing awareness that Jesus helped others and that Jesus is a special person.

Self

Babies and toddlers can also understand that:

I am a person.
We give opportunities for each child to hear that God made him, God planned for him to grow, God gave him different parts of his body so that he can do different things; he begins to sense that he is special because God made him; we allow him to begin to make simple choices when appropriate (like which book to look at or which toy to play with).

Family

Babies and toddlers can learn that:
I have a family.
Each child becomes aware that God made families; they hear about ways that Christian family members show their love; they associate warm feelings with their family. (It needs to be said here that the whole subject of family life raises many questions and problems in these days of fractured families. We want to teach God's plan and intention for families accurately, yet sensitively. See 'Happy Families?' p.18.)

Church

Babies and toddlers learn that:
People love me and take care of me at church.
We help each child feel loved, cared for and secure at church; we help each child enjoy being at church.
People sing and talk about God and Jesus at church.
We provide opportunities for each child to hear teachers sing and talk about God and Jesus.
There are lots of things for me to do at church.
We provide a variety of learning activities for each child.

The Bible

Babies and toddlers can begin to understand that:

The Bible is a special book.
Each child has opportunities to see and touch the Bible.
The Bible tells about Jesus.
We provide opportunities for each child to hear stories about Jesus when the Bible is used.

Others

Babies and toddlers can begin to understand that:

People love me and take care of my needs.
We help each child become aware that other people take care of them.
I am aware of other people.
Each child becomes more aware of other people around them and enjoys being with other people.

Two and three year olds

God

Two and three year olds understand that:
God made people.
We help each child become aware that God made them and others.
God loves people.
Each child hears that God loves them; they become more aware of ways that God shows his love for people.
God wants people to love him.
Each child hears of how people show love for God.
People talk to God.
We help each child express thanks to God; we give opportunities for each child to hear their teachers talk to God, and for them to talk to God.
God wants people to love and help each other.
Each child hears about ways that people can help each other; we provide opportunities for them to help others.

God made the world.
Each child becomes aware that God made plants, animals, earth, sky, etc.; we provide opportunities for them to explore things God made.

Natural world

Two- and three-year-olds can also understand that:
God made the world and he provides food for people and animals.
Each child hears about the plants and animals God made; we help them associate God's name with nature.

Jesus

Two and three year olds can add to that understanding by learning:
Jesus was born, he grew, he had a family who cared for him.
We help each child associate the birth of Jesus with Christmas; we help them realise that Jesus grew up and that he was part of a family.
Jesus loves people and wants people to love him.
Each child will hear that Jesus loves them and other people, and will hear Bible stories about the way Jesus showed his love for people; they will hear about people in the

Bible who loved Jesus, and about people today who love Jesus.

Jesus wants people to love and help each other.

We provide opportunities for each child to hear about ways people help each other; we provide activities that enable them to help others.

Self

Two and three year olds can learn that:

I am growing and I can do many things.

Each child becomes more aware that God planned for and helps him to grow; he associates his ability to do things with God.

I am a special person.

Each child discovers that he is special to other people and that he is accepted and loved by others; he becomes more aware that God loves him and that God made each person special and different.

Family

Two and three year olds learn that:

God planned for family members to love and help each other.

We help each child understand that being part of a family is God's plan for people.

Other people are in my family.

We help each child to feel that they are a significant person in their family.

I can help my family

Each child becomes aware of ways they can help their family.

Church

Two and three year olds can learn that:
I have friends at church.
We help each child be aware of friends at church who love them; each child will feel happy and secure with these people; they will feel that they are a significant person at church.
People at church help others.
We provide opportunities for each child to hear Bible stories about people who helped at church and to hear of ways that people help at church today; we give each child opportunities to help at church.

The Bible

Two and three year olds can learn that:
The Bible has stories and verses about God, Jesus and people.
We help each child have an increasing desire to hear stories from the Bible.

Others

Two and three year olds learn that:
Other people love and help me.
We talk to each child about the ways other people care for them.
I can love and help others.
We help each child to learn ways that they can be kind and loving to others.

Four and five year olds

God

Four and five year olds can learn that:
God cares for people.
Each child grows in their understanding that God provides and cares for people.
God can do things that people cannot do.
Each child has an increased awareness that God can do things people cannot do.
God wants people to worship him and thank him.
We help each child understand that God wants people to worship him (read the Bible, pray, sing, tell him we love him); we provide opportunities for them to worship and thank God, because God is good.
God wants people to talk to him.
Each child becomes aware that they can talk to God any time and any place and that God hears our prayers any time.
God wants people everywhere to learn about him.
Each child is more aware that God wants people to learn about him.

Natural world

Four and five year olds learn that:

God made sun, moon, stars, snow, rain, wind, day and night.

Each child grows in their understanding that God showed his love by making the natural world.

God wants people, animals and plants to grow.

We provide opportunities for each child to see how plants, animals and people grow.

God wants people to care for the things he made.

Each child becomes more aware that the things God made need care, and that they can help care for them.

Jesus

Four and five year olds can learn that:

Jesus is God's Son.

Each child will develop more awareness that Jesus is God's Son and that God showed his love by sending Jesus.

Jesus helped people because he loved them.

We help each child begin to understand that not only did Jesus help people in the Bible who needed his help, but Jesus loves and helps them, too.

Jesus can do things that people cannot do.

Self

Four and five year olds go on to understand that:

I am important to God, others and myself.
We help each child realise that not only is he important to God and others, but to have a sense of self-worth also.

I can make choices.
We provide opportunities for each child to make choices when appropriate, and help him express his feelings, attitudes and actions positively through those choices.

I can take turns and share.
Each child is helped to share and take turns with others.

Family

Four and five year olds can move on to understand that:

God wants people to live, work and play together in families.
We help each child to understand this in the context of their own family situation.

Each person in a family has their own possessions and jobs to do.
Each child begins to understand that others in their family have things that belong to them, and that different family members have different responsibilities.

The Bible has stories about families.
We give opportunities for each child to hear Bible stories about families that love and help one another.

Church

Four and five year olds also understand that:

At church we sing songs, use the Bible and learn about God and Jesus.

Each child becomes aware of the importance of the things we do at church.

Going to church is important.

We help each child understand that being part of a church is what God wants for people.

People at church have different jobs to do.

The child becomes aware that although people at church have different kinds of jobs to do, we all work together to help other people learn about God and Jesus.

People go to different church buildings.

We help each child learn that there are other churches besides theirs.

The Bible

Four and five year olds can also understand that:

The Bible is an important book.

Each child sees teachers and other adults at church handle and use the Bible frequently.

The Bible helps us to know how God wants us to live.

We help each child to hear stories and verses from the Bible that tell how to treat other people; we help each child become aware that Bible truths relate to their everyday life.

Others

Four and five year olds move on to learn that:

I can be considerate of other people.

We help each child become aware that each person has feelings.

Some things belong to me and some things belong to others.

We help each child to grow in their understanding that not everything belongs to them.

God (Jesus) wants people to love and help each other.

Each child has opportunities to learn ways that they can help others.

People are alike in some ways and different in some ways.

We help each child understand that although we are alike in many ways, God has made each one of us different.

God planned for us to have friends.

Each child grows in their understanding of what it means to be a friend.

Perhaps these lists are much longer than you expected them to be! You may have doubts about whether any child under five can learn all of this. It might even seem more sensible to stop reading now, rather than try to wade any further into this impossible task!

Yes, the lists are long and fairly comprehensive. So is the Bible - there is a lot to teach! Of course, each child will grasp these foundational areas at their own pace and according to their own capabilities. And even the brightest of children would not be able to recount each of these truths as we have written them here. Remember, learning is not measured by what children can say, but by what they understand and can put to use. It is very nice to *hear* children say, 'God wants us to love and help each other,' but it is far better to *see* them help another child with a difficult puzzle or assist the teacher in putting the bricks away at the end of the session!

It never ceases to amaze me just how much young children can and do learn. The task of building these foundational truths into their lives is daunting but it is also very rewarding to see them growing up knowing the love of God in their lives.

I said this list was not exhaustive but you may feel exhausted just reading through it! On the other hand, you may think of many things I have left out. If you think through these truths, you will see that many of them overlap. Some of them we will teach directly through our words. Others will be 'caught' by the children as they grow.

In our success orientated society, where what we have done is so often measured, this process of building biblical foundations doesn't easily fit. Though it is our goal to give children a strong grounding in these areas, most of them will not be able to say concretely what they have learned. True learning is not being able to repeat what we tell them. It is the ability to apply what we have shown them. Most three or four year olds have an amazing capacity for memorisation. They can hear what we say and repeat it back but the Bible tells us quite clearly that the mark of our faith is not knowing what the Bible says; it is doing what the Bible says. We want to teach children these foundational truths in ways that enable them to see how the Bible applies to their lives.

At long last, the foundations are finished. The channels have been dug, the concrete has been poured and set. Now it's time to start building the walls! We know how children learn; we know what children can learn. In the following sections we will work that out in terms of practical activities.

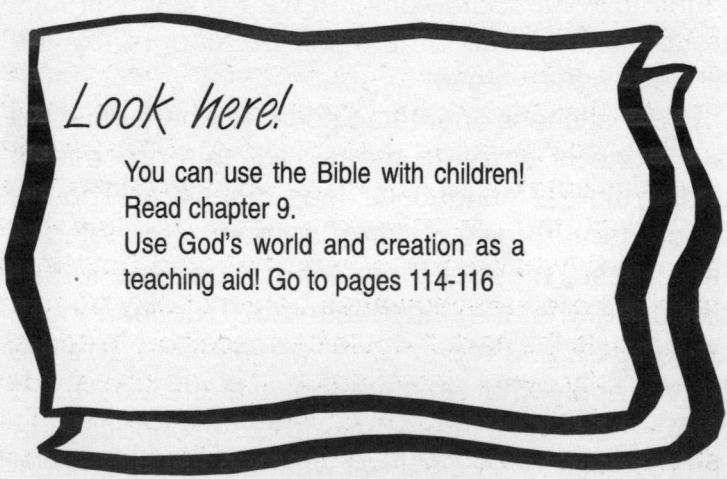

Look here!

You can use the Bible with children! Read chapter 9.
Use God's world and creation as a teaching aid! Go to pages 114-116

8 Teaching through play

If you ask adults for their impressions of 'Sunday School' they may well describe children sitting on chairs in rows, facing a teacher. If they are advanced thinkers, the teacher may even have a story board or flannelgraph next to her! (Sunday School teachers always seem to be pictured as female, of course!)

Let's replay that scene, taking into account all that we have said about how children learn. Think about a room where there are a variety of play activities on offer. Think about children moving from one area to another, choosing what they do next. Think about teachers (women AND men) interacting with children as they play, helping them to understand biblical truth.

The most effective (and fun!) way I have found to communicate the biblical truths we have talked about is through the use of various activities. How many activities, what types of activities and how many teachers are involved varies tremendously from one situation to the next. It would be impossible to address specifically every kind of setup. We will look at a few basic principles and at activities in general. This should give you enough information to work out how to do this in your situation.

The room itself

The physical facilities of most churches leave a fair bit to be desired when it comes to space and suitability for babies and toddlers. If there is a room at all, it may be too small or crowded with equipment used by other groups. We may often be frustrated by inadequate buildings but we have to do the best we can with what we've got. Think creatively. Could homes of nearby church members be used for older groups so rooms in the church can be used by the youngest children? Can halls be sectioned off to allow division of age groups? If there are no separate meeting rooms perhaps Sunday worship could be all-age in style and groups could meet during the week for age-appropriate teaching. There are rarely simple answers. Sometimes we have to try different things until we find out what works.

Let's assume, however, that you have a room to meet in. What you put in it will vary according to the age span you are teaching and how much space you have. Here are some suggestions for basic equipment you may want to have for each age group, whether you are in separate rooms or all in one room:

Babies

Choose various rattles that can be easily cleaned. Since many children will come into contact with them and will put them in their mouths, it is better to avoid fabric toys that collect germs. Wash or wipe rattles with disinfectant regularly. Small board books are good for teachers to look at with babies. If you have space, a bouncing seat or a baby gym is useful.

Toddlers
Good standard equipment includes: stacking and nesting toys, simple shape sorters, items for kitchen and home play, a doll and cradle, books, simple puzzles and wooden bricks.

Twos, Threes and Fours
The same things suggested for toddlers can be added to as children grow. The variety of home play items and kitchen 'equipment' will be greater, puzzles will have more pieces and books will have more words. In addition to wooden bricks you may want to have 'construction' type toys such as Duplo, stickle bricks, etc. (Lego may work in a room where there are no babies or young toddlers. If you have a mixed age group, don't use it. Pieces get lost or put in tiny mouths!)

One of the pitfalls for many churches is that there is a tradition of people passing on their old toys 'to the creche'. What this usually means is that there is a collection of tatty, old-fashioned things, many with pieces missing or broken parts. These may be dumped out on the floor each week and don't make a very inviting welcome for young children. Too many toys can be overwhelming. The choice is too great and children don't know where to start. It is better to have fewer items that are intact rather than a vast array of things, none of which work properly. I have noticed that in churches people are loathe to throw anything away. Most church cupboards need a fairly major sorting out by someone who is not afraid to say, "I think we can get rid of that"! Money used to buy good quality, basic items as outlined above is money well spent.

How many activities to provide?

This is dependent on space and the number of teachers. If your group is babies and toddlers, you may have a number of things to play with but only one or two activities that require specific teacher input, such as water play, sand play or simple painting. If you have birth to four in one room you may have a broader variety of things to play with and still provide two or three 'special' activities each week. ('Special' means things you don't normally have, as opposed to complicated or time consuming for teachers to prepare!) If you have one or two other teachers who can interact with the younger children, then you can involve yourself with older ones, perhaps bathing a doll, washing the dishes, gluing collages, playing with dough or making instant whip. These kinds of activities cannot be left unattended when there are babies and toddlers in a room. If you have the luxury of having a narrower age band in your room, the kinds of activities you can provide will depend on numbers of children and teachers.

In any room, there are some activities I would provide every week to give continuity and because they are always popular: home corner ('dolls and dishes'), bricks, books and puzzles. All of these can happen with a teacher moving around the room, watching the different areas, helping and interacting with children as possible. Another teacher can supervise the 'special' activities. If you have three teachers, you may be able to have two 'specials' available at once. If you can only do one teacher led activity at a time you would need to let everyone participate who wants to, then put it away and perhaps a bit later get out another activity.

Who does what activity?
I am asking this about the children, not the teachers! Some people teach in a style that means everyone does one activity for a while, then that is put away and everyone moves on to the next thing. This approach works better with school age children who are used to learning in this way. I find that pre-school age children respond well to making choices. Some have short attention spans and flit from one area to another every few minutes. Other children may sit and play with bricks for 20 minutes before moving on to something else. Some may even spend the whole time in one area! Always ask these children if they want to do something else, particularly if there is an art activity which they can take home. If they say no, honour that and let them get on with what they are doing. In this way they learn to make choices in a non-threatening situation with minimal consequences. The worst that happens is that at home time they don't have a painting to take. You can remind them that when they were asked about painting they were busy doing something else. This helps them to learn about choices and consequences in a way they will soon recover from! Later on in life they will need to know about this in much more serious ways.

The beauty of having a variety of activities, even if it is only two or three areas, is that it respects children's different likes and styles of play. When a child has chosen to play in a certain area it is more natural for teachers to chat about spiritual things than when a child is grumpy because they are being 'forced' to do something they don't particularly enjoy.

Let's now take a look at some of the different activities you might be able to provide. Most of these have older toddlers and two to four year olds in view. Some of these are things you might provide every week, others are special things that may link to the teaching theme.

Bricks/construction toys

 A good set of wooden building bricks is in my top five of most used items.

Even babies can grasp bricks, and older babies/young toddlers can begin to stack them or tap bricks together to make a noise. As they do you can say, "Thank you, God, for John's ears to hear the tapping sound" or "Thank you, God, for Sarah's eyes to see the red brick".

As three year olds work together to build something you can say, "The Bible says 'be kind'. When you share the bricks you are being kind. You are doing what the Bible says."

If a child knocks over someone's tower you may be able to help them understand that other people have feelings: "Mark, when you knock Andrew's tower over it makes him feel sad. Please do not do that again." While this kind of statement doesn't mention God or the Bible, it certainly reinforces a biblical view that other people matter.

If you have children over two you may want to alternate other construction toys in addition to bricks. You could put out Duplo one week, stickle bricks the next and so on. It is not necessary to go out and buy these things. Bricks alone are fine. But if you can afford or have access to these items, they make a nice addition.

Puzzles

A puzzle is more than just a wooden tray with lift out pieces.

Anything that requires a child to find the connection between two things is a puzzle. This is good, as wooden puzzles can be expensive. Home-made puzzles cost next to nothing and be more fun because they are different.

Cut three inch squares out of a variety of colours of paper, several of each colour. Let children sort them by colour. Three year olds can sort by shape, so cut out circles, stars and triangles as well.

In winter, cut out pairs of mittens in different colours and let them match them up.

Add a puzzle to the home corner by bringing a small basket of different coloured socks for the children to sort into pairs.

Pick up two advertising leaflets at the supermarket and make a matching puzzle by cutting out the same pictures of food from both of them. Mount one set of pictures on a large piece of card. Glue the others to small, individual pieces of card and let children match the sets.

Provide buttons or beads for three and four year olds to sort. Supervise carefully because of the small pieces involved.

If the puzzle links with the teaching theme you may be able to tell a child part of the Bible story as they do the puzzle. If it doesn't link, you may say something like, "Emma, you can sort the different shapes. You are big enough to know so many things. God planned for you to grow and learn new things. He loves you." This simple statement helps a child to see that even the most ordinary things of life (like working a puzzle) are not outside God's care for us.

Home Corner

The home corner provides security for children as it contains elements that are familiar to them. As children look after the dolls and pretend to cook they develop physical, mental and social skills.

A home corner need not have elaborate, expensive equipment for children to enjoy it. In fact, sometimes simple, basic items allow for more creative play. If you don't already have the items and don't have the budget to buy them, you can make them. Here are some things you might want to include:

Dolls and beds

Choose your dolls carefully. Often people donate dolls and you end up with a motley assortment of rather dishevelled looking dollies. If you are able to buy dolls, choose ones with plastic bodies and no hair so they can be washed. Steer away from soft dolls. As nice as they are to cuddle, they are breeding grounds for germs. If you don't have a doll bed you can make one out of a wooden crate. Make sure it is sanded smoothly and put a few small blankets in it. You can even use a sturdy, shallow cardboard box.

Plastic dishes

You don't need to have all the fancy extras that are often advertised. A simple set of plates, cups, bowls and spoons is plenty. Check them regularly to make sure there are no cracks or jagged edges where handles have come off cups.

Cooker

Again, wooden crates come in handy. Turn one up on end to create a hob. Alternatively, make one out of a cardboard box. Stuff it full of wadded up newspaper then tape it shut. This will stop it getting crushed. You can draw hob rings on the top of it. These are the basics of a home corner. If you have the money and the space, you might add a sink, a cupboard or an ironing board. From time to time you might want to add extra things to fit the theme of the session or to add interest:

- Extra items for baby care such as nappies and plastic bottles.
- Dressing up clothes (Adult clothes are so big that children may struggle to manage them. Clothes that fit older children are usually better.)
- Real saucepans and wooden spoons from home.
- A washing basket with clothes to sort.
- A small suitcase with items to pack.
- Real fruits or vegetables for looking at or tasting.

As children play in the home corner there may be opportunities to talk about families, about helping or about taking turns. As a child plays, you could tell them a sentence or two about the Bible story, or share one of the Bible verses for that session.

Books

Books are valuable for any age of pre-school children. Even babies who can focus their eyes will enjoy sitting on a teacher's lap to look at the pictures in a book. Because children learn by repetition, they often enjoy the same book over and over.

When buying books, look for sturdy books with simple pictures and not too many words. In this teaching context you are not likely to be able to sit down and read a ten minute story to a child, so fairly simple words and phrases are better. Obviously the difficulty will vary with the age you are teaching.

Books can get expensive and you can't always find one that relates to your teaching theme. Home-made books are perfectly acceptable and sometimes children enjoy them even more. Here are some ideas.

Buy an inexpensive photo album of the type where the clear cover peels back from the page. You can make a book on any theme by cutting out pictures from magazines, or even drawing them if you are able. It only takes a few minutes to make a book like this, and the next week you can lift the pictures out and put new ones in.

For a smaller book that can be more easily handled by a baby or toddler, make the book on sturdy card. You can often find pieces of plain cardboard and cut them to the size you need. Glue the pictures on the pages, punch two holes on the left side of each page and tie them together with wool, ribbon or string.

Babies who are able to sit up and hold things enjoy a 'picture cube'. This is like a book only there are no pages to turn. Use an empty tissue box of the taller, more square type. Stuff it full of crumpled newspaper so it won't collapse. Cover it with plain or pale coloured paper. Glue a different picture on each of the six sides or attach pictures with several strips of sellotape, covering the picture completely so they can't rip it off.

Let older pre-schoolers work together to make a book. If, for instance, the teaching theme relates to families, let each child have a piece of paper. Have pictures of people cut out of catalogues or magazines available for them to glue, as well as crayons, pencils or felt tips for them to draw. When they have made a picture 'about their family' (which may look nothing like human beings at all!) ask them to tell you something about their family that you can write on the page. You may have to prompt with questions about what they like to do with their dad, mum, grandma, etc., whether they have any pets or what their family likes to eat. Write one sentence on each child's page. Punch holes and tie the book together as above. You can read it at group time. Children love to see a book they have helped to make.

 **Nature**
The world that God has created is a wonderful teaching tool.

What seem to us the simplest aspects of nature are fascinating for young children. At times you may be teaching specifically about God making the world but even when you are not, it is good to have some sort of activity relating to nature every couple of weeks. The possibilities are numerous. You could start with these:

In season, bring fresh flowers from your garden for children to look at. Older ones can arrange them in a vase. (Flowers that have been arranged and re-arranged several times are pretty dilapidated by the end of a session, but the point is in the doing, not the finished arrangement!)

For babies to hold flowers safely you may want to put a few in a clear plastic jar with a lid or in a small, clear plastic bag that can be sealed. Of course, this would need to be supervised at all times.

If you don't have flowers in your garden you can get slightly 'out of date' flowers from a florist very cheaply. If you go in a few days before you want them and explain what you are doing, they will often save flowers for you that would normally be discarded. To you the flowers may look 'past it', but the children won't notice.

Collect shells at the seaside and let children look at them, play with them in a bowl of water or bury them in a bowl of sand.

Water play and sand play are both ways of enjoying nature.

At harvest time bring a large pumpkin. Children enjoy rolling it around, sitting on and patting it (it makes a nice sound). You could even cut it open so the children can see all the seeds inside it. If you have access to an oven you could even toast the seeds and let the children taste them. Make sure you notify parents of this in case of allergies.

Bring a small pet for the children to see. A goldfish swimming in a clear jar (with a lid!), a hamster, gerbil or bird in a cage or even a rabbit, if it is tame enough, are sources of wonderment to young children. Always notify parents by a note on the door as well as verbally in case their child is allergic to animal fur.

 Provide a variety of leaves in different sizes, shapes and colours for children to look at. This seems more mundane to us as adults but children are just learning about the vast array in nature so they are interested.

Place a selection of fruits or vegetables with different colours, shapes and textures on a tray for children to handle. Choose more robust varieties that will not be squashed by curious hands.

The list could go on and on. As children observe nature there are many opportunities to thank God for all he has made, including us.

 **Music**
Young children love music. I have rarely met a baby or young child who did not respond positively to singing or musical instruments.

Some people are reluctant to sing with children because they feel they cannot sing well. Not being very tuneful may matter when you are working with older children or adults, but it doesn't make any difference with pre-schoolers.

Some people may hesitate to use music because they do not have access to a musical instrument to accompany their singing. Again, young children are not bothered. They enjoy instruments but are just as happy singing without them.

Every now and then you can use music as a teaching activity by doing something special but singing songs can be part of all your teaching. First let me suggest some special ideas, then we'll talk about singing anytime and anywhere.

Bring a portable cassette player and have background music. When we are trying to pass on spiritual life, the lyrics of most pop music probably aren't helpful so find a bouncy kids praise tape, a reflective instrumental tape or even some classical music.

Sometimes children enjoy waving scarves and 'floating' to gentle music or waving flags and dancing to more exuberant praise music.

Provide homemade instruments for children to play, such as shakers or sticks to tap together. You can make a string of bells by sewing bells onto a short length of wide elastic and making it into a bracelet to slip onto a child's wrist.

Have someone bring in a guitar, string or wind instrument and play it for the children. Make sure the person is happy for the children to touch their instrument and even have a try making a sound with it. (This is not the place for someone's prized Stradivarius!)

Children enjoy music as a special activity but you can sing with them every week, not just in group time, but as you interact with them in play. Music is excellent for reinforcing biblical truth. Here are four points to think about in relation to songs for very young children:

♫ *Note range:*
Keep it fairly limited. Children can't sing very high or very low. Actually, neither can most adults so it works well for both teachers and children.

♫ *Tune and rhythm:*
Simple melodies and rhythms are best. They are easy for you to remember and easier for children to learn. Also, simple melodies don't take the emphasis away from the words.

♫ *Words:*
The words need to be literal, concrete and in the vocabulary of young children. We have already looked at the need to avoid the abstract or symbolic in what we teach. This affects the words we sing as well as the stories we tell. A song probably needs not to have too many words. If you are wanting to convey a particular truth, a few lines are enough.

♫ *Actions:*
Many people think that children's songs need to have actions. In fact, some research indicates that children find it difficult to concentrate on two things at once. (I suspect most adults do, as well!)

If children are singing a song with actions they are likely to be thinking more about the actions and less about the words they are singing. In fact, they may do the actions but not sing the words. This may be fun but it means the song doesn't teach them any truth.

A song that takes into account the points we have already looked at does not need to have actions to be enjoyable or effective.

One exception to this is songs where the action does what the words describe, like clapping hands or tapping feet. Songs that describe actions that children can do are fun to sing. They may not even mention God but they are part of the child's development so are valid even in the teaching context. Action songs or rhymes like this are very useful in settling children for the Bible story.

If you think carefully through these four headings you may feel there are not many songs left! I find that for a specific teaching theme there isn't usually a song anyway so I just make up songs. Before you skip this bit because you aren't a composer, please hear me out. It is easier than you think to make up songs. If you are musical, you can think of your own simple tunes. If you are not musical, use well-known nursery rhyme type tunes and put in the words that convey what you want to teach. Let me show you:

If the Bible story is from the book of Ruth, you could sing these words, repeating the tune of the first two lines of 'Twinkle, twinkle little star':

Ruth and Boaz had a boy,
Baby Obed was his name.
Grandma Naomi lived with them,
they were a happy family.

If your theme is the Bible itself, you could sing these words to 'Here we go round the mulberry bush':

The Bible is a special book,
a special book, a special book.
The Bible is a special book,
it tells us about Jesus.

With some thought and practice, you can come up with many different songs. Some will be specific to a teaching session. You will sing them to a child as they play with bricks. The child won't know the song but they will listen and enjoy. You may never sing the song again. Other songs with a more general theme may be used many times.

Music is such an effective tool for teaching children that it is worth the effort to become comfortable with using it. Whether it is just with one child, a small group doing some activity, or the whole class at group time, a simple song can often be part of the process of passing on biblical truth and living faith.

Art

This is probably the area most people think of first when working with pre-school children. 'Give us some craft ideas!' is often their plea.

Before we look at ideas, it is important to think through the purpose of using art in teaching. Why do we provide an art or craft activity? Is it to make something that illustrates the Bible story? Is it to give the children something to take home that their parents will be impressed with? Is it to fill time in the session?

I don't believe that the purpose of art is any of these. Art allows children to express themselves creatively and have a sense of accomplishment. Much of what is done as art and craft with pre-schoolers fulfils the first agendas suggested rather than the second. When planning an art activity keep these guidelines in mind:

Simplicity
The activity needs to be something the children can do mainly for themselves, with only some guidance from the teacher. If you have to do most of the work for them, the activity is too difficult.

Freedom
One of the most common mistakes made in the area of art with very young children is having a finished product in mind. Adults come up with marvellous ideas for illustrating the Bible story and may spend hours cutting out various shapes and pieces that then need to be put together in a certain way. ('Put tab A into slot C. Here's one I made earlier!) The teacher then has to stand over every child to make sure they do it 'the right way'. The finished product may look nice but it is not the child's work, it is the teacher's. Simple art activities that allow a child to create something of their own are more effective. For young children it is the process rather than the finished product that is most satisfying.

Encouragement
Provide activities that allow you to encourage every child. We may feel that the art work needs to illustrate the teaching in some way so we give children a picture about the Bible story to colour in or glue things on. Many young children do not yet have the manual dexterity required for colouring within lines. If they think that you want the picture to look a certain way when it is finished, they may not even be willing to try because they know they can't do it. Even at this young age they do not want to fail.

Adults may say something like, "Let's see who can make the best picture," in order to encourage the children to do well. Unfortunately, this creates the impression that some work will be more acceptable than others. Children will encounter competition soon enough. Surely as we seek to pass on our faith we would want to affirm each child's efforts, no matter what the finished product looks like. "You were careful not to spill the paint, Joanna. You remembered to wipe the brush against the side of the pot." "Richard, thank you for taking turns with the glue spreader while you made your picture." "Sarah, I can see that you worked very hard on your picture. I hope you had fun using the fingerpaints today." Commenting on the process may encourage children more than praising the finished product.

Another common mistake is asking "What is it?" Some three or four year olds may set out to draw a picture of a lion or of their grandmother. Others are simply using crayons for the enjoyment of the experience. A picture doesn't have to be anything to be valid. Nor does it have to look like what the child says it is. To a three year old, a mass of scribbles may well be them playing at the park. A person with purple hair and orange eyes is not incongruous to some four year olds. Obviously, most toddlers or two year olds aren't capable of making a recognisable picture. This does not matter at all. We are not there to say, "That is a good picture, James." A more appropriate response might be, "Thank you, God, for James' hands so he can hold the crayons", or "I'm glad we can do fun things at church. Thank you, God, for our church."

Creativity

As adults, we often gain satisfaction in terms of end results or finished products. Young children are not like that. Their pleasure and learning is in the process of doing and making, not in the product which results. It is good to provide art materials, give some guidance about how to use them and let the children get on with it. It is better to give them time to be creative and not worry so much about what it looks like in the end. It is easy for us to feel that their parents will judge the effectiveness of our teaching by what kind of art or craft product the child goes home with. We must seek to provide experiences that are of more benefit to the children than to us.

Practicality

If you want to use a new idea, try it at home first! You will then be able to see if it actually

123

works, if the children will be able to do it, how thick the paint might need to be, etc. Many of the art activities we do with children are fun for grown-ups, too. Have your turn at home, then you will be even more enthusiastic about it during the session.

Choice

 Some children will always want to make use of the art materials, others may rarely, if ever, want to do so. It is good to give every child the opportunity, but let them choose whether to participate or not. Obviously, with the style of teaching we are looking at here, the children will not all do the art activity at the same time. They will take turns, and you will need to keep track of who has had a turn and who hasn't. If Jonathan is busy with a puzzle when you ask him the first time, ask him again later. You may want to say, "Jonathan, I am going to put the paint away in a minute. If you want to do some painting today, you will need to do it now because we will not be getting the paint out again later." The choice is then his. If he says no, and then wants to have a picture to take home, he will learn that his choices have consequences. This is an important part of development that many adults do not seem to have come to terms with!

Giving children a say about participating in art as well as the other teaching activities honours their own interests and preferences as well as helps them to learn about making wise choices.

These guidelines may seem numerous and complicated, but in fact, they allow for much more ease and simplicity in both preparation and in the teaching session itself. There are dozens of possibilities, and when you have tried them all, you can start again since children learn through repetition! Here are a few ideas to get you started:

Painting

Paint is a wonderful medium for young children. It is also messy so make sure children wear aprons. Have a bowl of warm sudsy water and a towel ready for clean up of hands! Paint at the easel; paint with cotton buds; with small squares of sponge held with pegs; use leaves as 'paintbrushes'; detach the ball of a roll-on deodorant bottle and fill it with paint for 'roller-ball painting'; roll paint-dipped marbles around on a piece of paper, cut to fit inside a shoe box for interesting patterns; or paint with household 'gadgets' like a potato masher, a pastry/cookie cutter or empty cotton reel. In addition to different types of painting, vary the size and shape of the paper you use. Paint on circular pieces of paper, triangles or long narrow rectangles.

Gluing

A huge variety of items for collage are fun and easy to work with: paper scraps in simple shapes cut from a variety of colours; fabric scraps; lace and ribbon scraps; lightweight nature items like leaves and small flowers; pictures cut from catalogues and magazines (these can fit a theme, like food, people, animals or trees).

Remember that the learning is in the doing so if children glue their pictures upside down, or glue paper scraps on top of each other or hanging off the edge of the page, it does not matter. Young children do need guidance not to use too much glue. One way to avoid big messes is to pour a small amount of glue into an empty film or yogurt pot and top it up if necessary. Glue spreaders are inexpensive to buy and you only need a few as you probably won't havemore than three or four children gluing at one time. (With young toddlers I find that I only have enough hands and eyes for one child at a time, plus the other one or two that 'watch' with their hands everywhere!)

Crayons

Sometimes it is good to give children just crayons and paper. Some will scribble, older ones might draw. Toddlers need to be shown that pushing the crayon across the paper leaves a mark. (The technical term for this is 'cause and effect'.) Resist the temptation to give them a picture to colour in. The majority will not stay within the lines anyway so they might as well make their own creation. Rather than colouring in a picture that illustrates the Bible story, you can tell them the story while they make their own picture. Three and four year olds enjoy making texture rubbings so provide leaves, corrugated cardboard or fine sandpaper for them to rub crayons over. Chunky crayons work best. Show the children how to turn the crayons on their side and rub across the paper.

These are a few suggestions, to keep you going for several sessions. Don't worry about linking the art activity to the teaching theme. This is occasionally possible (e.g. a collage of pictures of people when the theme is families) but it is often difficult, and can appear contrived.

Passing on truth happens as you talk with children while they participate, tell them Bible verses or part of the Bible story, sing to them or relate what they are doing to spiritual concepts. "Kieron, you are big enough to stand and paint at the easel now. God planned for you to grow." "Michael, you are being kind when you share the glue spreader with Sarah. The Bible tells us to be kind. You are doing what the Bible says."

Using the Bible

We have looked at various teaching/play activities we might use and how we can communicate biblical truth one-on-one as we do them. The next chapter will look specifically at 'group time', and telling the Bible story to the whole group at once. In this section, however, we will look at using the Bible specifically in all our teaching so that babies and young children not only hear about what it says, but they see it and touch it for themselves.

I never cease to be amazed at most young children's keenness to know what the Bible says. They seem to soak it up eagerly and are at a wonderful stage when they simply accept that it is true. If only we could find a way as adults to come with that child-like attitude to God's Word.

We have already looked at foundational truth that pre-schoolers can learn. Obviously, there is much about the Bible that is complicated to understand and difficult to live out. There is also much that is beyond the mental comprehension of young children. But there is certainly plenty that is very straightforward and we know exactly what it means. Ephesians 4:32, for example, says, "Be kind to one another". I don't know about you, but I don't need a trained theologian to explain that one to me! Psalm 92:1 tells us it is good to say thank you prayers to God. That's not an intellectual challenge either. (It may be a spiritual challenge to put these into practice. I don't have any trouble understanding what God is telling me to do, though I may struggle to actually do it!)

Rather than focussing on the parts of the Bible that pre-schoolers are not yet ready for, let's concentrate on passing on to them the vast parts of the Bible they *can* understand.

Many of the stories in the Bible, both Old and New Testament, show us how God wants us to live. Others help us to understand his love for us or tell us about Jesus. Using these stories with pre-schoolers helps them to relate biblical principles to actual happenings. As they make this connection, they can learn to translate that information into everyday living. What a great thing for them to grow up knowing how to do!

Introducing the Bible

Where, then, do we start? How do we use the Bible with very young children?

Babies

It might be most helpful if we start with babies and progress from there. This will help give a framework, based on the development of the child physically, mentally and spiritually.

Parents and others are keen to talk to babies from the moment they are born. We tell them that we love them, that they are beautiful, or we talk to them about who we are and what we are doing. In other words, it is natural for us to tell them those things which we feel are important, even before they begin to understand. This is the way they should learn about the Bible - naturally, and from the beginning.

A newborn baby hears you when you say, 'I love you. The Bible says that Jesus loves you, too'. As you greet a baby in your room at church, he can hear you say, 'Good morning, Thomas. I'm glad you came to church today. The Bible tells us that Jesus went to church with his family. You have come to church too.' No one knows at what point Thomas begins to understand these words so we use them from his earliest days.

As you read these examples of things we can say to even the youngest of babies, you may dismiss them as simplistic. They are simple, not simplistic. They are, in fact, very profound. The problem is, we imagine them being said in that phony, sickly sweet voice that so many adults use when talking to babies. As we talk to children about the truths of God's word, we must use a warm, natural voice. There is no need for a put-on tone that implies insincerity.

As we meet the physical needs of babies we can relate that to the Bible. If you are giving a baby a bottle, you can say, 'You are enjoying your milk, Jodi. The Bible says that God gives us things to enjoy. Thank you, God, for Jodi's milk'. (1 Tim. 6:17) As Jodi learns to focus her eyes, you can sit with her in your lap and hold the Bible open. As she looks at it, you might sing, 'The Bible is a special book, it tells us Jesus loves us'. (This is another chance to make up your own tune!) You might also open it to 1 Samuel and say, 'The Bible tells us about a boy called Samuel. His mother took him to the big church at Shiloh so that he could help teacher Eli. Samuel was a helper at church'. For a young baby, these kinds of things are a good introduction to the Bible. They help them to understand that the Bible is about familiar things. This relates the Bible to everyday life rather than consigning it to irrelevance.

As babies reach the age when they can sit by themselves, you may want to sit next to them and show them pictures in the Bible. If you do not have a Bible with suitable pictures, you can use your own Bible. Provide a picture to illustrate what you are talking about. For example, you may have some pictures of birds. You can place these next to the Bible. As a baby looks at the pictures, you can say, 'These are birds. The Bible says that God made the birds. Look at all the different kinds of birds God made'.

If you are looking at a picture book of animals, you may be naming the various ones and imitating their sounds. As you come to a picture of a sheep, you could say, 'In the Bible we read about David. He helped his father by looking after the sheep. He found them green grass to eat, and water to drink'. Again, this reinforces the truth that the Bible has to do with our lives every day.

It is good for babies to hear about people in the Bible. A few sentences that convey a particular theme are sufficient. When they are older they will hear and remember whole stories about biblical characters. In the beginning it is enough that they hear about real people doing real things that they can relate to.

Toddlers and above

Somewhere around eighteen months to two years children start to listen to and take in very short stories. When this happens we can begin to use brief, simple stories from the Bible. We can tell them a few sentences of a story as they are involved in different activities. If there is some form of group time, they can hear the story again then.

Toddlers need to hear Bible stories and also Bible verses and thoughts that relate to what they are doing. Some verses are simple enough in vocabulary and structure to use as direct quotes. Ephesians 4:32, mentioned above, is one example. Another is Proverbs 17:17, 'A friend loves at all times.' We can use the verse to help children understand about being kind or being friends. Other factual verses give children helpful information. Matthew 2:1 says, 'Jesus was born in Bethlehem.' Matthew 19:14 says, 'Jesus said, "Let the little children come to me".'

Other verses in the Bible communicate important truths, but the words are beyond the understanding under fives. We can paraphrase those verses into language that is on their level. One example is Psalm 122:1. The NIV says, 'I rejoiced with those who said to me, "Let us go to the house of the LORD".' If you say that to a three-year-old they will want to know what 'rejoice' means and does the Lord's house have an upstairs like mine and are we staying there for tea?

A three year old might better understand the real meaning of this verse if they hear, 'I was glad when they said, "Let's go to church".' For a younger child an even simpler way to communicate the essence of this verse might be, 'I like to go to church'.

Many adults are impressed when young children memorise Bible verses. They think that the children are 'learning the Bible'. Perhaps it is more accurate to say they are learning to quote the Bible. I think we would be true to the message of the Scriptures if we say that God is more concerned that we understand and obey the spirit of the Bible than be able to quote the letter of the Bible without true understanding.

Most adults would gladly agree that we need to tell children Bible stories in language they can understand. Rephrasing Bible verses, without changing their intended meaning, is exactly the same principle. The most important thing is to help our children grow up to see that the Bible is alive and makes a difference to their lives now. I would rather see my own children demonstrate the characteristics described in the Beatitudes (Matthew 5) than be able to quote them from memory. (Of course, when they are old enough to understand the words, it would be nice for them to live them *and* memorise them!)

Hopefully this rather lengthy explanation will help you understand why, in this section on 'Using the Bible', many of the examples cited do not directly quote the Scriptures. The words may not be those you find in the NIV or even the Good News Bible but they convey the meaning intended. Some other examples of paraphrasing Bible verses are given at the end of this section.

As children reach three or four years of age they can understand and listen to greater detail in Bible stories. During activity time it may be appropriate only to tell a small portion of the story for that day. At group time they can hear the whole story. They will listen and understand more if they have heard one or two sentences from the story during the session.

Three and four year olds can also understand more Bible verses and thoughts. They may be able to repeat them after you have said them. It is good to encourage this but not in any way that implies that a child who can say a verse is better or more clever than one who can't. Children will be helped to know and love the Bible when it is used in positive ways, rather than in 'competitive' ways.

It is good to have the Bible as available as possible to children during the session. If you are working with babies or toddlers, they can only use it with supervision so it cannot be left lying on the floor. With children above toddler age you may want to place the Bible in one of the activity areas each week. Open it to an appropriate verse and lay a marker made of coloured construction paper on the page. On the marker write the reference and the verse, either as it is, or paraphrased if that is more appropriate.

Bible activities

The Bible can be an activity in itself. Most children are very interested to know what the Bible says. Here are a few suggestions.

Make several markers out of different colours of paper.

On each one write a reference and the verse or a paraphrase of it. Put them in the correct places in the Bible, with about two inches of the marker sticking out at the top. As a teacher sits with the Bible, children will wander over to see what he is doing. Let a child choose a marker, then open the Bible and say, 'The Bible says. . .' and read the verse. For a two year old, this may be enough. A three or four year old may want to repeat the verse, either with the teacher or alone. Some children may want to talk about the verse. Let the children take turns choosing markers. It doesn't matter if several children choose the same one. If this keeps happening, though, you may want to slide a marker right down inside the Bible after it has been chosen. Let the next child choose a different one and so on, until all the markers have been chosen. You can then slide them all up again and start over. Let this go on as long as children are interested. Some may come and go after only one verse, others may stay for 10 or 15 minutes. When interest seems to wane, the teacher can put the Bible away and involve himself in another activity area.

Play a matching game with markers.
For each marker you make for the Bible, make another blank one the same colour. Let a child choose a blank marker, then find the matching colour in the Bible. This can be managed by some older two year olds. They may not be able to say their colours, but they can match by sight. For three and four year olds, you may want to make the matching of a different type. You might make all the markers the same colour but at the top of each one put a sticker. Each one could have a different shape or colour. Make two of each so that the children can match them up. You may be able to find matching pictures, such as flowers by obtaining two identical gardening catalogues.

Throw a bean bag to choose a marker.
For each coloured marker you make, cut a circle of the same colour. The circle should be three to five inches in diameter. Spread the circles out on the floor and let the children take turns gently throwing a beanbag. Whichever circle it lands on (or nearest to!) is the colour they must find in the Bible. Again, if the same colour keeps coming up, you may want to remove a circle once it has been landed on, until all circles are gone.

These 'games' stimulate interest, and help the children really enjoy seeing what the Bible says. They encourage participation, even amongst the more shy children because there are no winners or losers. A child can play without any fear of failing.

Choosing Bible stories

Taking into consideration all that we have said about how children learn and understand things, what would be the aims and/or criteria for a Bible story for under fives?

It must be fairly simple.

It would involve events that under fives know about or can relate to.

It would illustrate a biblical principle that they can understand.

It would be concrete, about real people and specific happenings.

What are some stories that would or would not fit in this framework?

Creation: This can be told simply. It may be best broken up into three or four stories over as many weeks. The story of creation involves things children know about - sun, moon, plants, rivers, animals and people. It helps them to understand that 'God made the world'. Although we do not know how God made the world, we emphasise all the things he did make. I have rarely been asked how God made these things. (Not by a child, anyway!) If a child did ask, this story illustrates another important truth. You could say, 'That's a good question. I don't know exactly how God made the animals. But the Bible tells us that God can do things people cannot do. You and I cannot make an animal, but God can and he did'.

Ruth: The story of Ruth staying with Naomi and finding grain to make bread teaches something important; families love and look after one another. This story has real people in it, can be told simply and is about something children know about - needing food to eat and taking care of people we love.

David and Goliath: What about this story? This is certainly an exciting story and it could be told simply. Beyond that, however, it does not fit the aims. It is about things that children under the age of five do not understand - a giant, slingshots, armies and killing. Although the story is real and concrete, its significance is symbolic; no matter how small and unimportant you may feel, God can use you. This is a wonderful truth but it is beyond the understanding of young children. There are details in this story which may be frightening or confusing to an under five. Giants are not generally portrayed in fairy stories as friendly. Although those giants are not real, this one was. We cannot say that it is just a story. Why would it be all right for David to kill someone? Killing doesn't make people happy. Why would God want David to do that? These questions are hard enough to answer when we can think symbolically and understand conceptually. Rather than raise them with under fives, perhaps it is better to leave this story until they can better grasp its significance.

The same difficulties would arise with some of the other 'popular' stories in the Old Testament, such as Jonah, Daniel in the Lions' Den, and Joshua and the

Walls of Jericho. These stories may be suitable for teaching older children but they may not be the best for teaching under fives.

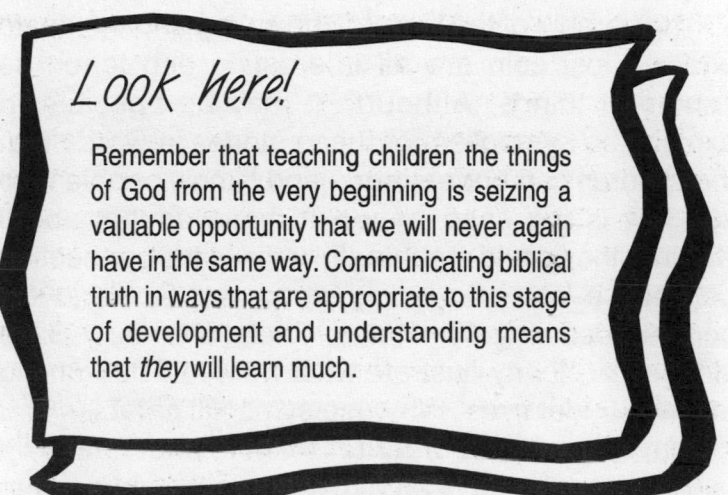

Look here!

Remember that teaching children the things of God from the very beginning is seizing a valuable opportunity that we will never again have in the same way. Communicating biblical truth in ways that are appropriate to this stage of development and understanding means that *they* will learn much.

New Testament: In the New Testament, there are many stories about Jesus that help young children understand how he loved people, that he did good things and that he told us how God wants us to live. In case you are thinking that this sounds like a fairly weak approach to who Jesus is, remember that under fives cannot understand about God as Father, about Jesus taking our place on the cross or about the revolutionary nature of what Jesus said and did. They can understand that Jesus made sick people well, that he taught us that God loves and takes care of the birds and he loves and takes care of us, that Jesus had friends (Mary and Martha are two we know something about) and that Jesus went to church.

The parables of Jesus are symbolic in their meaning and are therefore difficult for under fives to benefit from. The wise and foolish builders is a great story but young children have no idea what foundations are - in life or in buildings!

The parable of the talents, the sheep and the goats and the lost coin are all interesting and teach us important things. Although it may be possible to explain the symbolism of these stories in words that the children can understand - and I know people who say this is the case - I would have doubts about whether they could meaningfully make the connection between a lost coin being found and God's joy at people becoming Christians. There are many Bible stories that clearly illustrate what we would be wanting to teach under fives. Why use symbolic parables that we have to adapt in order for them to understand?

The parable that is an exception is the story of the kind man (known to us as the Good Samaritan). It illustrates being kind to others. The more subtle issues in the story, like racism and stuffy religiosity, are better left for a later age. You can use the main facts, though, and begin it by saying, 'One time Jesus told the people who were listening to him a story about a man who...'

New Testament stories about Paul, Aquila and Priscilla, Lydia, Philip and others all illustrate different biblical principles. Each of these people loved Jesus and told others about him. The story of Paul's conversion may be too difficult but there are many stories of him working with others, going to different places telling about Jesus and writing letters to his friend (Timothy, in particular) that under fives can learn from.

When choosing Bible stories and teaching aims for under fives, remember that it is not necessarily the most well known stories that are the best. Stories such as King Josiah repairing the church, and David and his friend Jonathan can effectively teach under fives important foundational truths.

Much of our Christian teaching today focuses on the New Testament and the more familiar stories and characters in the Old Testament. Using some of the more 'obscure' stories as well can give under fives a good foundation for later understanding how God deals with his people. When we read the passages in order to condense the stories, we may find that God teaches us some things or helps us to see them in a new way.

At the end of chapter 10, on page 173, you will find some suggested stories for under fives. As you become familiar with how they are used to teach spiritual truth, you will be able to choose and condense other Bible stories yourself.

The Bible is a very special book. It is a history book, a poetry book, a hymn book and an exciting narrative. It is the only book that claims to be living and active. It is a relevant guide for all our lives. It helps us understand the God who made us, loves us and is faithful to us. The Bible reveals Jesus, our Saviour and our Lord. May God help us to teach our children to love and respect, and, most importantly, to live out this most holy word.

Paraphrases for under fives

Verses
Genesis 1:11 'Then God said, "Let the land produce vegetation: seed-bearing plants and trees on the land that bear fruit with seed in it, according to their various kinds." And it was so.'

Genesis 1:27 'God created man in his own image, in the image of God he created him; male and female he created them.'

Paraphrase
God made trees. God made fruit. God made grass. God made flowers. God made people.

Verse
Exodus 20:12 'Honour your father and your mother, so that you may live long in the land the LORD your God is giving you.'

Paraphrase
Love your father and mother.

Verse
Job 37:14 'Listen to this, Job; stop and consider God's wonders.'

Paraphrase
Think of all the wonderful things God made.

Verses
Psalm 71:23 'My lips will shout for joy when I sing praise to you - I, whom you have redeemed.'

Psalm 33:1 'Sing joyfully to the LORD, you righteous; it is fitting for the upright to praise him.'

Paraphrase
I will sing happy songs to God.
It is good to sing thanks to God.

Verses
Luke 2:52 'And Jesus grew in wisdom and stature, and in favour with God and men.'

Luke 4:16 'He went to Nazareth, where he had been brought up, and on the Sabbath day he went into the synagogue, as was his custom. And he stood up to read.'

Paraphrase
Jesus grew up. Jesus had friends. Jesus went to church.
Jesus read the Bible at church.

Verse
John 15:12 'My command is this: Love each other as I have loved you.'

Paraphrase
Jesus said, 'Love each other'. Jesus loves you.

Verse
Acts 10:38 '...how God annointed Jesus of Nazareth with the Holy Spirit and power, and how he went about doing good and healing all who were under the power of the devil, because God was with him.'

Paraphrase
Jesus did good things. Jesus went to many places and did good things. Jesus made sick people well.

Verse

2 Corinthians 1:24 'Not that we lord it over your faith, but we work with you for your joy, because it is by faith you stand firm.'

Paraphrase
We work together.

Verses

Colossians 1:3 'We always thank God, the Father of our Lord Jesus Christ, when we pray for you . . .'

1Timothy 6:18 'Command them to do good, to be rich in good deeds, and to be generous and willing to share.'

Paraphrase
We thank God for you.
Be ready to share. It is good to share.
God wants us to do good things.

Verses

1 Peter 5:7 'Cast all your anxiety on him because he cares for you.'

1 John 4:10 'This is love: not that we loved God, but that he loved us and sent his Son as an atoning sacrifice for our sins.'

Paraphrase
God cares for you.
God loves us. God loved us and sent his Son.

This list is not exhaustive. It only gives an introduction to the way verses can be paraphrased, in addition to the examples cited in earlier paragraphs.

Choosing a Bible for use with under fives

In recent years a variety of Bibles have been published with children in mind. The layout and the pictures reflect this decade rather than the 1950s. These attempts to make the Bible relevant and accessible to even the youngest of children are to be commended.

With such a wide choice of Bibles on the market, it is important that we choose carefully. Some of the modern Bibles use cartoon-style pictures. Although bright and attractive, they are not very realistic. They may not help us in trying to teach children that the

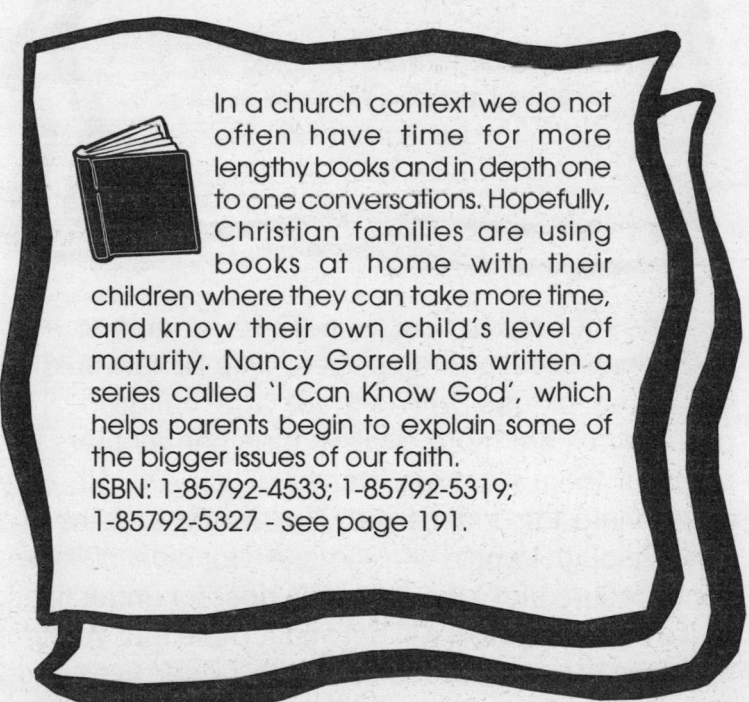

In a church context we do not often have time for more lengthy books and in depth one to one conversations. Hopefully, Christian families are using books at home with their children where they can take more time, and know their own child's level of maturity. Nancy Gorrell has written a series called 'I Can Know God', which helps parents begin to explain some of the bigger issues of our faith.
ISBN: 1-85792-4533; 1-85792-5319; 1-85792-5327 - See page 191.

 Bible is about real people in real places. Some of the 'Bibles' produced for under fives are not actually Bibles but are books of Bible stories. These may be very helpful for use in the home, though at church we may want to use a 'whole' Bible. Children get used to seeing it as we use the same one regularly.

The *New International Children's Bible* was published some years ago. It is a special translation

Look here!

The who, when, where, what and how of group times. Do you know about them? If not turn to pages 149 - 153

designed for children ages 6-12 to be able to read and understand for themselves. This Bible would be excellent for use with school age children. The pictures in it are more realistic than some others but many of them illustrate stories which are not very appropriate for under fives, like Jonah and the big fish. Although I would recommend it for older children, I am not sure that it would be the best for under fives.

It may be that you will not find a Bible that you feel has suitable pictures for use with under fives. You can use your own Bible with the children for marking verses and paraphrases. You may be able to find pictures to illustrate the Bible stories you use. If not, you can use the Bible without pictures. This is preferable to using pictures that do not clarify or reinforce what you are teaching.

Many books that retell Bible stories are published. While they may not always be the stories we use at church, they are great to use at home, where parents can reinforce that the stories from the Bible are true. Sometimes children like to hear the words of the story with no comment. Other times the stories can be used to teach important principles of Christian living. See pages 188-189.

10

Group Time

Group time with under fives can be very productive. It has the potential for building relationships, developing social skills and reinforcing and further teaching the Bible theme for the session. But it can be disastrous! Working with young children is unpredictable at the best of times. When they are all sitting together in a group, you never know what will happen next. Sometimes it's the things they do, but more often, it is the things they say.

I have heard many revelations about what has gone on in some of the homes during the week. I've also been on the other end of that when my own children's teachers have come to me and said, 'We heard all about you dropping the milk jug on the floor this morning!'

Once I was talking with a group of three year olds about things we like to do, and having fun. 'What do you like to do?', I asked. With total sincerity one little girl said, 'I like to pick my nose'. The children may have wondered why I suddenly had a choking fit!

Group time is not without its risks, but the potential benefits outweigh these considerably. The best insurance against embarrassing moments is being prepared. As we understand the who, when, where, what and how of group time, we can approach it with greater confidence and enthusiasm.

Who?

Opinions about what age is appropriate for group time may vary. Certainly you would expect to be having such a time with children three and above. I have used some form of group time with two year olds, and even with toddlers.

Many factors may influence at what age you begin trying to provide some type of group experience for children. If you have a room with mixed ages you will have to think carefully about whether you can actually manage group time. If you have more than one teacher you may be able to use part of the room for group time with the older ones. You may have a group of two year olds with very mixed levels of maturity. Some may be able to cope with group time, others may not. You may decide to start with only two or three minutes and slowly increase it to seven or eight minutes.

The length of time you have for your teaching session may also affect how you structure things. If you have an hour, you will not have any trouble fitting in meaningful group time. If you only have 20 to 30 minutes, you may feel that the younger children will benefit more by continuing teaching activities for the whole session.

In the section about what to do in group time, we will consider ideas for children as young as toddlers. Below that age, one-to-one interaction between babies and teachers is probably the most effective means of teaching spiritual truth.

When?

The best time for group time tends to be at the end of the session. There are a number of reasons for this:

It allows children time beforehand to expend their energy in productive ways.

It allows for much good teaching to happen during activity time. This makes children more receptive to the theme or story because they may have already encountered it in the various activities. Of course, there will not always be natural opportunities to share some of the Bible story in every activity area every week. Having group time ensures that each child has a chance to hear the Bible story.

Group time at the end means that the room can be tidied from activity time - helping to put things away is part of learning too.

Having group time when the children have finished their other activities means they are not looking around at what they want to do after group time. It also means that they can concentrate better because they are not thinking of the artwork they left half-finished, anxiously wondering when they will be able to get back to it.

Group time seems to fit most naturally at the end of the session. If, for various reasons, you must have it some other time, it can still be equally valuable.

Time scheduling

Making the most of teaching time on Sundays is important, whether it is twenty minutes or an hour.

Finding the time schedule that works best for you may only come through trial and error. The way you divide your time depends on many factors - the number and ages of children, room size, the number of teachers, and the amount of time you have.

Those who teach the babies and youngest toddlers are the least affected by the length of time. If time is short, it may be appropriate to provide only one new or different activity each week, in addition to the regular things you have. If you have 30 minutes or less, I would recommend teaching through activities only and not trying to fit in group time with children up to the age of about two and a half. For older toddlers and children over two, you may want to think in terms of having two 'new' activities each week.

If you are teaching children between two and a half and five, and you have half an hour or less, you may want to think of trying 20-25 minutes of activity time followed by a brief group time. Perhaps you could ask the children to do only the minimum of clearing away. Although it is important for them to learn to help with this, if your time is limited, it may be better used in activities and group time. If you find that it is too rushed, you may want to use only activities and ensure that one activity each week provides an opportunity for using the Bible story with the children who are involved in it. You may want to make the Bible the centre of an activity area and through the use of pictures or music make that area a place for 'mini' group time.

When time is short the temptation is to keep the children in a group the whole time, possibly only providing an art activity which involves all the children doing the same thing at the same time. Although this may be easier for the teacher, it may not be best for the children. I would still want to see at least two, and probably three, choices of activity where meaningful teaching occurs, followed by a brief group time.

If you have a longer time, 45 minutes to an hour, you can easily allow for teaching through activities, time for putting things away and group time. If you have an hour for teaching, you can allow 40-45 minutes for activities. This may sound like a long time, but with a variety of interesting activities and well prepared teachers, it goes quickly. (Occasionally I have days when the time seems to drag and I think my watch must have stopped, but these are few, and are usually more to do with me than with the children.)

However long (or short!) your time may be, you can provide meaningful teaching for under fives. Don't be afraid to experiment with different schedules. Try one for several weeks. If it doesn't seem right, try something else. If you continue to provide good teaching even through transition, the children will feel secure. They will not suffer unduly from your attempts to get it right.

? **Where?**

If you have a room with babies up to five year olds, you may find that it is helpful to take the older ones out of the room for group time. Even a quiet hallway might enable them to concentrate more easily. In general, though, the best place to have group time is in the same place you have activity time. If the room is small, it may be necessary to move things to the edges to make enough space.

If you have child-sized chairs, you may want to use them for children three and above. Chairs are certainly not necessary though. Children don't mind where they sit. It is only teachers whose legs may get a bit stiff on the floor!

If the children are sitting on the floor, it is generally better for the teacher to sit on the floor. I have made an exception to this when I have taught a large class of children. Because there were about twenty of them, I found it was easier for them all to see me if I sat on a low chair, rather than on the floor.

Sitting the children in a circle is usually the best arrangement. If they are in rows, the ones in the back cannot see. Children often need assistance arranging themselves into some kind of circle. A teacher other than the one who is leading group time can help with this or it can be made into a game. We will look at some ideas for this under the 'What and how?' of group time.

What and how?

Considering who group time is for and when and where it should be is like building a skeleton. Looking at what we do and how we do it puts flesh on these bones. Group time may have several components and these vary in length according to the age of the children. We will look at the different possibilities, then at how we might put them together to make an effective group time.

Movement songs or rhymes

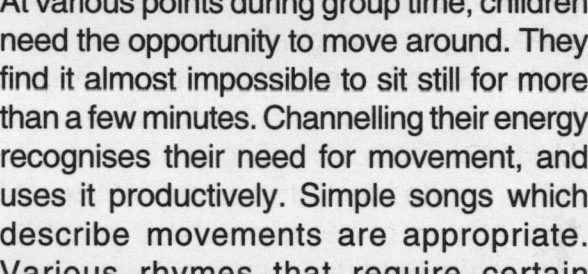

At various points during group time, children need the opportunity to move around. They find it almost impossible to sit still for more than a few minutes. Channelling their energy recognises their need for movement, and uses it productively. Simple songs which describe movements are appropriate. Various rhymes that require certain movements are valuable, too. They not only direct energy but they are part of physical development. At the end of this chapter there are a number of suggested songs and rhymes.

'Name' songs and games

Children love to hear their own name said or sung. All the children I have ever worked with respond well to a simple song that uses their name. You may go around the circle singing to each child, 'I have a good friend, X is his/her name'. Some of the children will sing with you, others may not. Or you might sing, 'I am happy, I am happy, X is here today'. (These songs can also be used when greeting a child at the beginning of the session or to any child during activity time.)

For three and four year olds you can play games that involve naming children. You might describe what a child is wearing and see if the children can guess who it is. You might name two children and ask them to swap places. (This is an excellent game for subtly separating 'troublemakers'!) Or you might name one child and ask them to name another child. Then the two change places in the circle. These are good exercises for a teacher's memory as it is important to make sure that each child's name is used!

Using the Bible

Most of the suggestions given in the section entitled 'Using the Bible' can be used during group time. If you have a large number of children, you may not be able to let them all have a turn at choosing or matching markers. You can explain that there will not be time for everyone to have a turn but that other children will have a turn next week. This is very difficult for some children to understand or accept but it, too, is part of the development process. (This is another time for teacher's memory to be sharp remembering from one week to the next!) If not all children have had a turn to participate in such an activity, you may be able to use it again at the very end, while waiting for children to be collected.

Conversation

Group time is an important time for talking *with* children as well as *to* them. Let them tell you about the different things they have been doing during the session. You may want to ask questions about the different activities that were available that day. 'Who painted this morning?' 'Did I see a new puzzle today?' 'I saw some children tasting something this morning. Who would like to tell me about it?'

It is a good idea to remind children to raise their hands if they want to tell you something. This may sound like school, but really, it is just good common sense and courtesy. If several children want to talk, you could say, 'Mark wants to tell us something now. After that it will be Alistair's turn, then Lorena's.' Some children will soon get into the habit of remembering to raise their hand. Other children are always bursting to talk and they have trouble remembering. A gentle reminder is often necessary. 'Aaron, I know you want to tell me something. It will be your turn in a minute. Stephen has raised his hand, and it is his turn now.' Many of today's children are hungry for conversation. Some of them do not have an adult who regularly wants to listen to what they have to say. For these children, not only is group time conversation important, but special care can be taken at other times to listen to them.

Conversation can be woven into all the elements of group time. You can talk about activities, about the story, about the theme for the day. Often children have something they want to tell you about - a special outing, a birthday party, or any number of things (like their mum dropping the milk jug!). It takes time to get the balance right between giving the children important opportunities to develop in conversation, and not letting that become the only feature of group time.

Bible stories

I believe it is important for children to hear a story from the Bible each week. You may not use a 'Bible marker game' with them each week, but they need to see the Bible used in group time. As the teacher tells the story, he can hold the Bible open on his lap to the correct reference.

Most children under five will not remember the details of a Bible story. That is okay. When they are older they will have time for remembering. Many years ago I told the story of the kind man (The Good Samaritan) to a group of three year olds. I later discovered that one little girl went home and told her father that we had a story about a man who fell off a donkey! So much for details! The important thing is not that they can recite the story later at home but that they hear a story related to a theme they can understand.

For example, if you tell the story of Ruth looking after Naomi, they will probably not remember the names unless they happen to know a child called Ruth or Naomi. They may not remember that she chose to stay with Naomi and helped her find grain for bread. The important part is the connection between the story and living out what the Bible says. I would far rather have them remember that God planned for families to take care of one another and to say thank you to God for their own families, than to remember that collecting grain is called 'gleaning'!

The Bible story is an essential part of group time. It helps children understand that the theme is not just some nice words that are a good idea. They are a good idea because they are from the Bible, they are God's words.

Other games

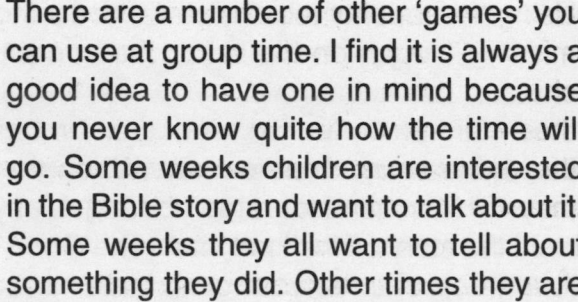

There are a number of other 'games' you can use at group time. I find it is always a good idea to have one in mind because you never know quite how the time will go. Some weeks children are interested in the Bible story and want to talk about it. Some weeks they all want to tell about something they did. Other times they are relatively quiet, or the things you have planned don't seem to spark their attention. It is always good to have more planned than you have time for. This allows for these fluctuations.

For toddlers and two year olds, the 'game' could be as simple as 'Can you?'. You ask them to do simple things. Can you clap your hands, stamp your feet, march around the room, wave your arms, etc? Or you may provide a simple activity, such as blowing bubbles for them or rolling a ball. Make the circle of children larger and roll the ball to each child in turn. You could sing, 'Roll the ball to X, roll it back to me'. Or you might want to give each child a small amount of playdough to squeeze and press.

For three and four year olds, you may want to have a 'feel bag'. In a cloth bag or an old pillowcase, place several familiar objects. The children take turns putting a hand in the bag and grasping an object. They can feel it in the bag and try to guess what it is without looking. Things like a small hairbrush, a toothbrush, a comb, a brick, a teaspoon, crayon, a small ball or a cotton wool ball would all be suitable.

Using the same types of objects, you can play 'what's missing?'. Arrange the objects on a tray and let the children name them all. Ask them to close or cover their eyes while you take an object away. Then ask them to look and raise their hand if they know what is missing.

A variation of this game for older three and four year olds is to place eight to ten objects on a tray. After the children have named them all, cover the items with a cloth. See how many of the objects the children can recall.

Involve the children in using their senses by playing 'I hear, I touch, I see'. Describe an object in the room by saying whether you hear it, touch it or see it, then give clues about it and see if the children can guess what it is.

Singing

In addition to songs that use children's names, you will want to use other songs. These may reflect the theme or relate to conversation. If the children have been telling you about all the things they have done that session, you may want to sing,

I like to go to church,
I like to go to church,
I like the happy things we do,
I like to go to church.

I am a musician so using songs spontaneously is easy for me. For those who are less musical, more planning is required. Have a song or two in mind for each part of group time. If it seems appropriate, use it. When the children are talking about something, such as the activities as mentioned above, I often say, 'I know a song about that'. I then sing the song to them and then usually say, 'Let's sing it again. You can sing it with me this time'. Some children will pick up a tune immediately. Others will try to join in. Some children will rarely sing themselves but they enjoy listening to you sing.

Music is an excellent tool. It helps children understand and remember things they have been learning. It involves even the most shy children, because they can participate by listening. It recaptures their interest and focuses their attention. And, in addition, it is good fun!

Prayer

Most prayers prayed by children in the context of group time will be thank you prayers. What a good foundation that is! Many adults would do well to pray more thank you prayers! It is good to allow those children who want to, to pray in group time. Their prayers often need some guidance.

After telling the Bible story about Jesus helping a blind man to see, you could say, 'I'm glad that Jesus helped the blind man see. I want to say a thank you prayer. Thank you, Jesus, that you loved people. Thank you for helping the blind man to see'. You may then want to ask if any children would like to say a prayer, thanking God for our eyes. If several children want to pray, try to give them all a chance.

This may sound very guided to you. Children need to learn to pray. They have heard many adults pray long, sometimes rambling prayers and they may do the same without some clear guidance. In the context of a group of young children, short, directed prayers are probably best. It is not necessary to ask children to close their eyes but you may want to suggest that sometimes. I tend to vary the way I pray. Sometimes I bow my head and close my eyes. Sometimes I look around at the children when I pray.

Children who are used to praying at home may tend to pray 'around the world'. Many have learned to do this at bedtime in order to stay up a bit later! If it appears that they are trying to pray for everything in one go, you may need to interrupt them gently and ask them to finish their prayer so that someone else can have a turn. Again, it is a question of getting the right balance between encouraging children to pray and at the same time, keeping other children's interest.

Now that we have considered what the elements of group time may be, let's look at how we might put them together. Firstly, we will consider some ideas for toddlers, then we will talk about three and four year olds.

Group time for toddlers

The term 'toddler' may be loosely defined as a child who has started walking - around the age of two. Children who are between two and three can fit into a group time designed for toddlers or into a group time for slightly older children. Where you put them depends on what the spread of ages is like and how you divide your groups. In a setting of mixed ages, you may want to combine these ideas for younger children with ideas for three and four year olds. Older children will accept some things that are aimed at toddlers and younger children can at least observe some elements designed for older children. As you get to know the children you teach, you will discover what works best. You will also find that as you move through the year the children mature and what you do in group time can 'grow' with them.

About ten to fifteen minutes before the end of the session, you can ask the children to help put things away. They require a large amount of help and supervision at this age, especially when bricks go in one bag, puzzles on a table and other toys in another bag! It is tempting just to do it yourself but helping to put things away is part of the teaching. It is the beginning of accepting responsibility. Once the toys are put away, you and the children can sit in a circle.

After a while, children learn the routine of things so they know that after they put things away, they sit for group time. I use the same purple blanket every week. The children in my class know that we sit there together at the end. With children this age, you may find it helpful to give them a drink of juice. This helps them to sit down and remain relatively still. It is not a must, however. You could use a simple movement song or rhyme to get their attention and settle them down.

You may find it best to tell the story fairly soon after the children are seated. After only a few minutes, their attention wanders and they get restless. You can make the most of sixty seconds of quiet to tell them the Bible story. This is best done without any props or pictures. If you show a picture or use a doll or puppet, they will be so busy looking at your 'prop' that they will not hear the story. After you have told the story you may have a picture you can show.

The story will be short and simple for this age. Read it through several times before the session and practise telling it without looking. The best way to hold the children's attention is by eye contact. Use variations in tone and volume of your voice to make the story live. It is not necessary to memorise what is written. Be able to tell it naturally, including all the important details. At the end of the story you may want to pray or sing a song. Not many toddlers would be able to articulate a prayer but it is good for them to hear the teacher pray.

You may want to use the rest of the time to look at the Bible, to sing songs or use movement rhymes. Always have some item planned for the last few minutes. In most churches, there is an approximate finishing time but it varies by a few minutes each week. Use that time productively with dough, a ball or a game. Teaching does not stop until the last child has gone. If you have only one or two children left, you may want to ask them to help you finish tidying the room.

With toddlers, it is better to err on the side of a short group time than to frustrate yourself and the children by trying to 'keep them entertained' for fifteen minutes at the end of the session. By the time the toys are put away and you sit down, you will only want to have about five minutes until the scheduled finishing time. In practice, this means you will actually have nearer ten minutes as you wait for parents and carers to collect children.

If you try group time with toddlers and find that it is more of a trial than a benefit, do not worry. Leave it and again in a few months. As long as you are teaching in the activities, they will not be 'cheated' by not having group time. We must remember that we want to build positive memories of times at church. We must be careful not to force children into group time before they are ready, simply because it fits within our adult definition of meaningful teaching.

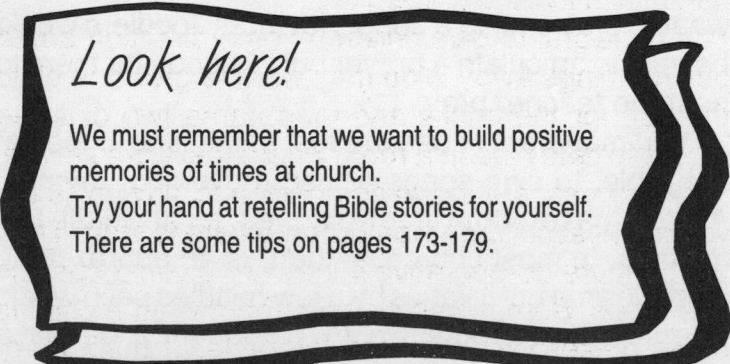

Look here!

We must remember that we want to build positive memories of times at church.
Try your hand at retelling Bible stories for yourself. There are some tips on pages 173-179.

Group time for three and four year olds

The transition to group time with older under fives will be much the same as for toddlers. They, too, need to accept the responsibility of putting away the items they have been using during the session. You may want to give children who are in the middle of an activity a warning that it is nearly time to tidy up. 'Heather, it will be time to put things away in a minute. You will need to finish your painting.' 'Ryan, it will soon be time to put things away. When you have finished your puzzle, would you please put all the puzzles together in a pile?'

Giving children a warning about the time is a courtesy. It shows them that you know that what they are doing is important to them. Suddenly announcing that everyone must stop what they are doing and tidy up can be extremely frustrating to a child who is engrossed in an activity. They may then come to group time feeling cross rather than looking forward to it.

It is helpful to give children some direction about putting things away. You may want to give one child the bag for the bricks and then name two or three others to help him. In a room where there are several activity areas, a general admonition to 'tidy up' is too vague. Most children won't know where to start. They will be more co-operative if they are given a specific task to do. Sometimes singing about what a child is doing makes his job more tolerable. (I think Mary

Poppins knew something about that - a spoonful of sugar helps the medicine go down!) You can let the children know it is time by singing, 'It's time to put the toys away, the toys away, the toys away. It's time to put the toys away and we can all be helpers' (to the tune of 'Here we go round the Mulberry Bush.)

Sometimes the children will come to group time and form themselves into a circle. If you always sit in the same part of the room, they become secure about where to go. From time to time you may want to make forming a circle into a game. You could suggest that the children stand together and as you sing their name they may come and sit down. It may help them if you move one place around the circle for each child so they know to come and sit in front of your feet.

You may want to lead them around the room in a movement song on the way to the circle. You could sing, 'It's fun to walk around the room . . . around the room with our friends' (to the tune of 'Here we go Round the Mulberry Bush' - a very useful tune!). You could add march, skip or hop.

Once you are seated together for group time, you can use any combination of the elements already suggested above. Every week you will want to have a Bible story, conversation and prayer. The other things you include will vary from week to week. Some weeks you may start with conversation, other weeks you may sing for a few minutes. When you are ready to tell the story, it is a good idea to let the children know that they need to be still and listen. I usually say something like, 'We have been doing lots of fun things and we have been talking together. Now it is my turn to talk for a few minutes. I would like you to listen to what I have to tell you'. This will help to cut down on interruptions during the story.

Have the Bible open to the reference for the story. Although you will not be reading directly from the Bible, this is a visual aid to help children know that the story comes from the Bible, not some other book.

Tell the story naturally, without referring to notes, if possible. Maintain eye contact with the children. As with toddlers, props are not necessary. In fact, they can be a distraction. Because children find it hard to concentrate on more than one thing at a time, they will watch the prop rather than listen to the story. School-age children can listen and look at the same time so they may be helped by the use of puppets or other aids. Under fives will take in the story and its significance more clearly if they hear it told simply and naturally, without any visual aids. You can hold their attention by varying the tone, volume and intensity of your voice. If you are interested in telling the story, they will be interested in listening.

When you have told the story ask some questions to encourage conversation about the story as it relates to the theme. Using again the example of the story of Ruth and Naomi, you could say, 'Ruth helped Naomi find food to eat. Who cooks the food at your house, Anna?' This will prompt conversation about providing food.

You could also say, 'Ruth wanted to stay with Naomi because she loved her and wanted to look after her. Robert, your mother and your grandmother love you and look after you. Who takes care of you, Michael?' (Remember that in conversations about home and family life it is helpful to know as much as you can about each child's situation. This enables you to include them without embarrassing them.) Many times this kind of conversation leads quite naturally into prayer.

After the story you may want to use any number of Bible activities, games or music. You could provide some musical instruments for the children to play. These may be bought or can be home-made, such as shakers and bells. It might be best to have only a few instruments and let the children take turns. If they are playing an instrument they probably won't be able to sing as well. If only some of the children have an instrument, the others can sing. Probably it is better to wait until after the Bible story to use instruments, as they tend to increase the noise level and it may be difficult to settle the children as quietly after that.

The key is a balance between security and variety. Children like to know that some things will be the same every week, hence the same location and always using the Bible with the story. But they also need some variety so you would want to use different games and sing a variety of songs, occasionally with instruments.

As with toddlers, it is good to keep the children involved in something even as they are being collected. If there are two teachers, one can stand at the door and quietly come and fetch a child from the circle as his parent arrives. This helps other children not to feel left behind and also uses time productively. I have found that things soon dissolve into chaos at the end if you do not have something for the children to be interested in.

The length of group time will depend on the age mix and maturity level of the children. Having a shorter time in order to accommodate younger children is more effective than trying to prolong it for the older ones. If the toddlers are fidgeting, the three year olds won't be able to concentrate anyway. For a group of three and four year olds you might think in terms of between ten and fifteen minutes. You will discover how long is best for the particular children you teach.

Before we conclude this section with some examples of songs, rhymes and Bible stories, a word about 'going home time' might be helpful. A good teaching session can end badly if the teacher never knows when to finish.

Some churches are very organised in their timetable and finish within five minutes of the same time every week. This is very helpful for teachers of all ages, because they can plan accordingly. Other churches, however, have a more 'laid back' approach. I remember talking once to a lady who was working with under fives. She was very frustrated because the children went out during the sermon. Sometimes this was only about 15-20 minutes, other times it was 30 minutes. It was almost impossible for the teachers to plan. How can you start group time 15 minutes before the end if you have no idea when the end is? You might plan to have activities for 30 minutes and find the parents turning up after only twenty.

If this situation sounds familiar to you, it might be worth talking to your church leaders about it. It is likely that they don't realise how difficult variable timing makes things for those who teach the children. Think carefully about your present situation, then come up with a few suggestions for how you might solve the dilemma. If you can talk or write to a leader very positively with possible solutions, they will be much more willing to help you. Perhaps if they understand what you are trying to do, they will try to be more disciplined about time.

If there is not an immediate solution to the problem of timing, you may have to adapt. Perhaps you could have group time in the middle, then let children return to activities until the end. This means, of course, that they will not easily be able to help with the tidying up. It is better to do it yourself, though, and use your time most constructively.

Another problem that arises relates to who collects the children and how quickly. From time to time, parents need reminding to come and collect their children first, then return to the worship area to chat to people. Some parents send a brother or sister to collect an under five. Occasionally, if I know the family and the circumstances, this may be appropriate, but generally I do not let children go with other children. I prefer to know that a child has gone with the appropriate adult. Very occasionally, I have had someone I do not know turn up at the door. They are family friends or relatives visiting for the day, and have come to collect a child while parents are talking. This has to be handled carefully. In all probability, they are who they say they are but, in these days, we have to be very careful of our children. I would rather embarrass myself than let a child go with the wrong person.

These issues related to the end of the session will be handled differently in each church. There is not necessarily a right or wrong way to do things. So much depends on the size and location of the church, and the way the time is structured. They are issues that must be thought through carefully so that teachers and leaders can work together to provide the best for everyone.

Sometimes the activity time goes brilliantly. The children respond eagerly to everything you do then group time is a disaster! Other times, the first part of the session is fraught with problems, but group time goes superbly. What a relief to know that the success of the morning does not depend on only one component.

Group time is an important part of the session, but it is not the most important part. Lack of teaching through activities is not made up for at the end by a ten minute group time. Nor does the occasional lacklustre group time negate what has gone on before but good teaching through activities can be built upon and reinforced by a group time that is designed to meet the needs of the children.

Movement songs

Almost any combination of movements can be sung.

Don't worry about using the songs over and over again. Children seldom tire of a good movement song. In fact, they may ask to sing it every week or more than once in any session! Here are some other words that children enjoy:

Snap, snap, snap your fingers,
Tap, tap, tap your toes.
Clap, clap, clap your hand
Then turn around while the music goes.

Hopping is fun, O hopping is fun,
Hopping is fun for everyone.
The more you hop, the better you hop,
So keep on hopping up and down.
(You can add marching . . . all around, skipping . . .
round and round, jumping . . . up and down)

♪ Movement rhymes

There are other options you can try. Here are four alternatives. There are many others. When you feel comfortable with these, try making up some of your own.

I touch my hair, my lips, my eyes.
I sit up straight, and then I rise.
I touch my toes, my knees, my chin,
Then quietly sit down again.

This rhyme involves opening and closing your fingers into a fist:

Open, shut them, open, shut them,
Hold them very tight.
(Squeeze both hands together.)
Open, shut them, open, shut them,
Shake them out so light.
(Shake both hands gently.)

Or you can vary the one above:
Open, shut them, open, shut them,
Give a little clap.
Open, shut them, open, shut them,
Put them in your lap.

Sometimes I'm tall,
(Stand and stretch arms above head.)
Sometimes I'm small.
(Stoop down low.)
Sometimes tall, sometimes small,
And sometimes, I'm just myself again.
(Stand normally.)

Bible stories

The following examples show possible ways of paraphrasing Bible stories to suit different age groups.

Since we have used the story of Ruth and Naomi as an illustration, perhaps we should start with that one. This would be appropriate for three and four year olds.

Ruth and Naomi (a)

A woman named Naomi lived with her husband and two sons in a country called Judah. One year there was not enough food to eat in that country. Naomi and her family were hungry. Her husband said, 'We will move to Moab. There is enough food there'.

So they went to live in a place called Moab. While they were there, Naomi's husband died. Her two sons got married - one married Ruth and the other married Orpah.

After many years, Naomi's sons died. Naomi wanted to go back and live in her own country. There was plenty of food there now. She set off with Ruth and Orpah but then she said to them, 'You do not need to come with me. Moab is your country. You can stay here - maybe you will be more happy'.

After they talked about it, Orpah decided to stay in Moab but Ruth said, 'I do not want to leave you, Naomi. I want to live in your country. I want to love God like you do. I will look after you. I am part of your family'. So Naomi and Ruth went back to Judah together. Ruth found grain for Naomi to make bread. Ruth took care of Naomi.

 If you want to use the story with older toddlers and two year olds, you can leave out some of the detail:

Ruth and Naomi (b)

Naomi's family were hungry. There was not enough food in their country.

Naomi's husband said, 'We will move to Moab. There is enough food there'.

So they went to live in Moab. While they were there, Naomi's husband died. Her two sons got married - one married Ruth, and the other married Orpah.

After many years, Naomi's sons died. Naomi heard that there was food in her own country now. She wanted to go back there and live. Orpah decided to stay in Moab. But Ruth said, 'I do not want to leave *you, Naomi. I want to live in your country. I want to love God like you do. I will look after you. I am part of your family'.*

So Naomi and Ruth went back to Naomi's country together. Ruth found grain for Naomi to make bread. Ruth took care of Naomi.

You could follow on with the theme of families caring for each other by continuing the story the next week.

Ruth and Boaz

Ruth went to the fields of grain to pick up the pieces that the workers left behind. She and Naomi would use the grain to make flour so they could bake bread to eat.

The field belonged to a kind man named Boaz. He saw Ruth gathering grain. 'You may come to my fields every day. I will tell my workers to let you gather grain. You will be safe in my fields.'

After a while, Boaz married Ruth. They had a baby boy. Grandmother Naomi was very happy. The women came to visit her and said, 'You must be very glad to have a grandson. God has taken care of you and Ruth. Ruth loves you and has looked after you well'.

The baby's name was Obed. Perhaps Grandmother Naomi helped Ruth and Boaz look after baby Obed. Perhaps she said, 'Thank you, God, for my grandson'. Naomi was glad that she had a family to be with.

 If you want to use this story with toddlers and two year olds try the following version.

Ruth and Boaz (b)

Ruth picked up grain from a field. She and Naomi would use it to bake bread that they could eat. The field belonged to a kind man named Boaz.

After a while Boaz married Ruth. They had a baby boy. Grandmother Naomi was very happy. The women came to visit her and said, 'You must be very glad to have a grandson. God has taken care of you and Ruth. Ruth loves you and has looked after you'.

The baby's name was Obed. Perhaps Grandmother Naomi helped Ruth and Boaz look after baby Obed. Perhaps she said, 'Thank you, God, for my grandson'. Naomi was glad that she had a family to be with.

This story below is for three and four year olds.

Jesus teaches about God's care (a) (Matthew 6:25-33)

Wherever Jesus went, people followed him. Many of them liked to listen to the things he said.

One day, Jesus sat outside, teaching the people. He said, 'Look at the birds in the sky. They do not have to work hard to make food. But God provides food for them to eat. He loves the birds, but he loves you even more'.

Then he looked at all the flowers growing in the field. He said, 'Look at all these flowers. They do not have to sew to make clothes for themselves. But even kings dressed up in all their best clothes are not as beautiful as the flowers. God loves the flowers but he loves you even more. God takes care of the flowers and he will take care of you too. The most important thing is for you to love God and do the things that please him. He will take care of you'.

 If you want to use this story with toddlers and two year olds try version b below.

Jesus teaches about God's care (b) (Matthew 6:25-33)

One day, Jesus was sitting outside teaching the people. He said, 'Look at the birds in the sky. God loves the birds, but he loves you even more. God takes care of the birds and he will take care of you'.

Then Jesus looked at the fields and said, 'Look at all the beautiful flowers. God loves the flowers but he loves you even more. God takes care of the flowers and he will take care of you. The most important thing is to love God and do the things that make him happy. God will take care of you'.

This story below is for three and four year olds.

Jesus and Bartimaeus (a)

Bartimaeus sat by the side of the road. He could hear the footsteps on the dusty road as many people walked by. He could hear the sound of their voices, talking and laughing but he could not see them.

Bartimaeus was blind. He called out to the people walking past him, 'What is happening?'

Someone told him that Jesus was walking past. Bartimaeus had heard about Jesus. He knew that Jesus could make people well.

'Jesus,' he called out, 'Jesus, please help me.'
Some of the people told him to be quiet but he shouted even louder, 'Jesus, please help me!'

Jesus heard Bartimaeus, and said, 'Tell the man who is calling to come to me'.

The people said, 'Quick, Bartimaeus. Jesus is asking for you'. They led him to Jesus. 'What would you like me to do to help you?' asked Jesus. 'I want to be able to see,' said Bartimaeus. 'It is good that you believe I can make you well', said Jesus, 'You can go now'. As soon as Jesus said that, Bartimaeus could see again. Bartimaeus had been blind. Jesus helped him to see again.

(This story lends itself to good conversation with three and four year olds. What is it like to be blind? Close your eyes and cover them with your hand. How do you think Bartimaeus would have felt after Jesus made him see? Do you think he would have been glad? These kinds of statements and questions help the children to understand the significance of what Jesus did.)

 Here is the same story told slightly differently for toddlers and two year olds.

Jesus and Bartimaeus (b)

Bartimaeus sat by the side of the road. He could hear but he could not see. He was blind. He heard the sounds of many people walking past him. He called out, 'What is happening?' Someone told him, 'It is Jesus. Jesus is coming this way!'

Bartimaeus had heard about Jesus. He knew that Jesus could make him see again. He shouted, 'Jesus, please help me!'

Jesus heard him and asked the people to bring Bartimaeus to him. 'What would you like me to do for you?' Jesus asked. 'Please, Jesus, I want to be able to see', said Bartimaeus. 'You knew that I could make you well', said Jesus. 'Now you can see'. As soon as Jesus said that, Bartimaeus was able to see again. Jesus had made him well.

These examples will help you to see how you can tell Bible stories accurately, but in language that young children can understand. Try rephrasing some yourself. Here are some suggested stories:

God made the world   Genesis 1

God made people   Genesis 1 and 2

Miriam helps care for baby Moses   Exodus 2:1-10

King Josiah repairs the church
and reads the Bible to the people   2 Kings 22-23:1-3

Jesus is born   Luke 2:1-7

Shepherds visit baby Jesus   Luke 2:8-20

Simeon and Anna see Jesus   Luke 2:22-40

Jesus goes to church   Luke 2:40-51

Four men take their friend to see Jesus   Mark 2:1-12

The man who said thank you   Luke 17:11-19

Jesus and the children   Matthew 19:13-15
       Mark 10:13-16
       Luke 18:15-17

A boy shares his lunch   John 6:1-13

Jesus visits friends   Luke 10:38-42

Paul works with Aquila and Priscilla   Acts 18:1-4

Philip tells a man about Jesus   Acts 8:26-35

Recommendations by the author

BOOKS

GOD MADE

Some books are great for use at church and at home. Titles that I recommend for pre-school children are the brightly coloured board book series: God made... published by Chrsitian Focus Publications:

God Made Me
(ISBN: 1-85792-2891)

God Made the World
(ISBN 1-85792-2921)

God Made Colours
(ISBN 1-85792-2913)

God Made Animals
(ISBN 1-85792-2905)

GOD GAVE ME

Teach pre-schoolers about the senses and about God with the God gave me series. A lovely chunky board book series which teaches children about the world they live in and their God who made it.

Touch (ISBN 1-85792-5602)
Taste (ISBN 1-85792-5610)
Sight (ISBN 1-85792-5629)
Hearing (ISBN 1-85792-5637)
Smell (ISBN 1-857925645)
Feelings (ISBN 1-85792-5653)

A Last Word

Teaching young children at church (and at home) is only a part of building for God's future, but I believe it is a very important part. We may never be able to measure the results of all our work in this area. Teenagers or adults who are committed to serving the Lord may not even remember those who taught and influenced them before they were five. My experience shows me, though, that among Christian teenagers and adults, the most mature spiritually are often the ones who have known the things of God from a very early age.

The children that you and I have in our charge as parents, teachers or carers, are growing up in a rapidly changing world. What do we need to teach them to equip them for the future? What do they need to know in order to fulfill God's purposes in their lives? How can we help them to grow up into men and women of God?

In our changing world there are very few certainties. As Christians we have an unchanging, faithful God, who has given us his word for our lives. What better foundation can we build into the lives of our children than to help them know, obey and love this Word?

Remember the vision we spoke of in the early pages of this book? That you and I might see a generation of children who have never known anything but to love the Lord? It will take a long a time to see the fulfillment of this vision. We may never know how many lives have been touched by our loving, consistent teaching. The measure of our service for God lies not in visible results, but in our faithfulness to what he has called us to do.

For many years my mother taught conferences in the United States for teachers of under fives in the church. She often used this little poem:

> *I saw tomorrow look at me*
> *through little children's eyes,*
> *and thought how carefully we'd teach*
> *if we were really wise.*

Through the young children we teach, you and I have an opportunity to touch and change tomorrow. May God help us to be faithful, and give us a passion for passing on a living, active faith to our children.

Janet Gaukroger

FOR ALL YOUR
PRESCHOOL NEEDS

BIBLE BOOKS

Little Hands Story Bible
by Carine Mackenzie

An excellent introduction to a wide range of Bible stories. Well written, with realistic illustrations and interactive questions throughout. An ideal first Bible for pre-school children.

SHAPED BOARD BOOKS

The Big Picnic
Feeding of the 5,000

A fun and innovative approach to telling Bible Stories to children. The simple facts are retold in a format that will delight both adults and children.

The Man on the Mat
The healing of the paralysed man

Another shaped board book which takes a well-known Bible story and retells it for young children. In durable board format this will be a favourite!

The Special Baby
The Birth of Jesus

This is a story that is not just for Christmas. A delightful stable shape this little book is an excellent way to retell every child's favourite Bible story. The angels, the shepherds and the donkey all feature... but the main character is Jesus - the very special baby!

God's Little Guidebooks
by Hazel Scrimshire

An excellent introduction to the teaching behind the Ten Commandments. This is a series of ten paperback mini books that young children will love collecting. There is one book for each of the commandments and two little characters Sam and Katy who discover what it means to follow God and obey him.

God made Animals,
God made The World,
God made Colours and
God made Me!

Four sturdy, toddler friendly, chewable,
endurable board books to give children
enjoyment and a knowledge of God, their
creator.

My First
Experiences

This is an excellent series for pre-school children. Each book features a different little boy and girl facing a new situation for the first time.

The children learn by discovering that these children trusted in God - so they can too.

Ideal presents for children in these specific situations or just excellent stories to give to a child you know.

My First Experiences teaches Bible truths simply and accurately. Children learn about life, the world and God. Scripture verses back up the teaching on each double page spread.

Children will also enjoy finding the small creature hiding in each picture.

I Can Know God

How do you begin teaching children about God, the Bible, faith - important Christian truths? Start at the beginning... with this unique Family Guide to the Christian Faith. The best place to teach very young children about faith and God is in the home environment and this is reflected in the series

I Can Know God.

Beginning with God

God, The Bible, The Trinity

ISBN 1-85792-453-3

Meeting with God

Creation, Jesus, Salvation

ISBN 1-85792-5319

Living with God

Worship, Heaven, Obedience and Prayer

ISBN 1-85792-5327

Bible Stories for Bedtime

Bedtime is a notoriously difficult time for parents of toddlers and pre-school children. Try this book for size. Bible Stories for Bedtime is a large format hard back book ideally laid out as a book to read to children. All the characters in this book learned about trusting in God. Your child will learn this too when you read God's word to them and pray the short simple prayers that conclude each story.

ISBN: 1-85792-4673

CHRISTIAN FOCUS

Good books with the real message of hope!

Christian Focus Publications publishes biblically-accurate books for adults and children.

If you are looking for quality Bible teaching for children then we have a wide and excellent range of Bible story books - from board books to teenage fiction, we have it covered.

You can also try our new Bible teaching Syllabus for 3-9 year olds and teaching materials for pre-school children.

These children's books are bright, fun and full of biblical truth, an ideal way to help children discover Jesus Christ for themselves. Our aim is to help children find out about God and get them enthusiastic about reading the Bible, now and later in their lives.

Find us at our web page:
www.christianfocus.com